INSIDE PSYCHOTHERAPY

Inside Psychotherapy

MARSHALL P. DUKE
Emory University

A. STEVEN FRANKEL
University of Southern California

MARKHAM PUBLISHING COMPANY / Chicago

MARKHAM PSYCHOLOGY SERIES

ALLEN, ed., *Psychological Factors in Poverty*
DUKE and FRANKEL, *Inside Psychotherapy*
MOYER, *The Physiology of Hostility*
MOSCOVICI, *The Psychosociology of Language*
SAHAKIAN, ed., *Psychology of Learning: Systems, Models, and Theories*

COPYRIGHT © 1971 BY MARKHAM PUBLISHING COMPANY
ALL RIGHTS RESERVED
PRINTED IN U.S.A.
LIBRARY OF CONGRESS CATALOG CARD NUMBER: 75–146016
HARDCOVER STANDARD BOOK NUMBER: 8410–5006–6
PAPERBACK STANDARD BOOK NUMBER: 8410–5014–7

To our families

Preface

Throughout the creation of this book, we have kept in mind that we were writing for three kinds of people: psychotherapy clients and potential clients, psychotherapy students, and psychotherapists. The primary focus of the book is, of course, the client.

Subjective experiences in psychotherapy (ours, our clients' and our colleagues'), as well as our research efforts, led us to believe that familiarizing the client with the therapy process by describing the procedures in general and reporting individual experiences would help the client. As a result, we became interested in research into mechanisms that could be used in a therapy situation to provide such aid.

Our research efforts suggested that typescripts of therapy interviews could provide this aid by giving the client a concrete insight into the process. He would know how therapy is conducted, what the process is about, and what to expect of the therapist. Research has shown the relationship between the client and therapist to be extremely important, for when a client and therapist share mutual expectancies about the therapy process, both the effectiveness of the process and the comfort of both the client and therapist are increased.

We feel that it is of the utmost importance that clients who read this book realize that the interview excerpts presented here are examples of how others have behaved in psychotherapy, and in no way are they intended to represent the *only* way to behave. Certainly, each individual has his own style—his own unique qualities—which must take precedence. Thus, not only should what is said in therapy go beyond the statements made by the clients in this book, but the way in which it is said may also vary. Our efforts are mainly oriented toward familiarizing the public with the process of therapy, thereby increasing the likelihood that the client and the therapist will share the same expectancies and providing models of appropriate behavior in the therapy situation.

For the student of psychotherapy, our efforts have been oriented toward providing a more concrete descriptive view of the process of therapy than most other sources have provided. The scripts are proposed as models for appropriate client behavior, but may also serve as models of appropriate therapist behavior. Certainly, it must be kept in mind that just as each client is unique, each therapist has a personalized approach to treatment; we do not contend that the therapists in these scripts have responded in the only appropriate way. Therapist style is often as important as client style, and these models should not be viewed as constraints upon such style. Nonetheless, in demonstrating ways in which other therapists have responded to clients with various types of difficulties, the scripts can serve as a valuable guideline.

For the practicing psychotherapist, we have attempted to provide a mechanism that will speed up the therapeutic process by increasing the concordance between therapist and client expectancies for treatment. By making the process of therapy more open and available to public scrutiny, we believe that many of the problems associated with what information should be conveyed in therapy and appropriate modes of conveying such information can be resolved.

Although some of the case material in this book has been drawn from actual clients, the names, times, places, and other identifying information have been changed drastically. Thus, any similarities to actual persons and circumstances are purely accidental.

The therapist has a great deal of latitude in using the book. Since not every client will have difficulties in all areas covered in the book, the therapist may request clients to read only selected portions. Other approaches might include using the scripts in the book as catalysts for discussion of certain problems. Therapists conducting research in psychotherapy will find the scripts useful in many ways, and can compare the effect of using them *vs.* not using them on progress in psychotherapy.

In sum, we are offering a way to make use of the findings of psychotherapy research in the psychotherapy process. These enterprises have too long been functioning separately, without a bridge between them.

M.P.D.
A.S.F.

Los Angeles, California
November, 1970

Contents

CHAPTER 1

Beginning Psychotherapy: How Therapy Works

A major object of this book is to clear up the misconceptions that surround psychotherapy, and thereby enable the individual who enters psychotherapy to achieve an understanding of how it works, what can and cannot be accomplished, and how progress can be aided and enhanced. For some people, the fears and concerns that these misconceptions have raised can be a problem more difficult than those that brought them to the therapist's office.

The mind has always been regarded with awe, fear, and a special reverence that is reserved for those aspects of man's existence that he cannot easily understand or control. Certainly, the terms "mental illness," "emotional problems," and "psychological difficulties" arouse far greater discomfort and fear in most people than the terms broken leg, appendicitis, or tonsilitis. Part of the reason for this is that a broken bone or an appendicitis or tonsilitis attack can be understood and treated in very concrete, specific ways. Further, these ailments are curable. When a person breaks a leg, for example, there is nothing mysterious about how to treat it: consult a physician, who will set the leg and place a cast around it. In a matter of weeks or months, the cast is removed and the leg is "as good as new." Moreover, the patient derives a good deal of comfort because he can point to his ailment and say "there it is—that's what is wrong with me."

An individual who has emotional problems is not so fortunate. The bases of his problems are not so easy to identify. It is almost impossible for him to point to something and say "there it is—that's what is wrong with me." Part of the problem is that while there is considerable agreement between physicians as to what causes tonsilitis, for example, there is not such a high degree of agreement between mental health workers as to what causes emotional problems. Further, it is very common for an individual to fear the worst about himself. Such a fear builds and grows stronger as he broods about his difficulties, and he often becomes convinced that he is "hopelessly crazy." When this conclusion is reached, he may become frightened that others will discover him—that everyone will find out—and that he will lose social, financial and personal security. The fear is compounded by the fact that many people believe that emotional problems are incurable, and that once an individual becomes emotionally ill, he can never be normal again.

Thus, the individual who experiences difficulties, regardless of what kind, may view psychotherapy treatment as an open admission that he is incurably insane or emotionally ill. When a friend, relative, clergyman, or family physician suggests that a person see a psychotherapist, one of the most common reactions is: "Why? Do you think I'm crazy?" The fear increases.

Thus, there is a range of reactions and feelings involved in entering psychotherapy. Several of these will now be presented. First is that of a twenty-five-year-old female who is making an effort to be as helpful as possible, despite considerable fear and embarrassment. The reader should remember that these excerpts are not designed to be imitated. Certainly, people are individuals, and their problems are individual as well. Thus, for the reader who is entering psychotherapy, these excerpts may be seen as attempts to clarify the ways in which material can be discussed productively in therapy. The important point to remember is that regardless of the nature of one's difficulties, one must try to be as honest and open as possible and to present material in the clearest manner possible. The following excerpt illustrates one individual's attempt to do this in therapy.

Therapist. Miss A., you look upset. What seems to be the trouble?

Client. I don't know, doctor. I really wish I did, though. I'm very nervous . . . can't seem to stop shaking. (Laughing nervously.) Oh, this is silly. I must look like a complete fool. I . . . I'm . . . I'm having some problems, and I thought I'd better see someone about them. It's mostly this nervousness, like the way I am now. Every once in a while I get this way, and I can't seem to stop it. I don't understand why it happens . . . I . . . it frightens me, doctor. Can you do something to help me?

T. Can you tell me more about it, Miss A.? For example, what kinds of things bring it on?

C. Well, let's see . . . I really don't know. It doesn't happen all the time. Maybe once every week or every two weeks. It doesn't matter what time of day it is or anything, except . . . well . . . I don't recall ever waking up feeling this way. The earliest it comes on is around ten-thirty or eleven in the morning. It can last all day sometimes, and once or twice it has lasted for two or three days. That's when it's the worst.

T. Can you remember the kinds of things that happen just before you have one of these experiences?

C. Well, I'm not sure . . . there have been so many of them . . . it's hard to say.

T. Let's just take this last time. What happened just before you became upset today?

C. Umm, I . . . I had an argument . . . that's right . . . I had an argument with my boyfriend. He called this morning to plan for the weekend, and we got into this big fight, and then I got nervous. You know, now that I think about it, I often get nervous like this when I get into fights or arguments. Do you think that has anything to do with my nervousness?

T. Perhaps. Can you tell me more about what happened today? Maybe we can get a clearer idea of just what does go on in your life that makes you upset.

C. Yes, I'll try. It's a little embarrassing, though. I mean, a lot of the things we argue about are fairly personal, and . . . well, it's hard to talk about them without getting embarrassed.

T.   Yes, I know that some of the things that bother people are very embarrassing, but such things are the most important to try and talk about.

C.   Yes, I suppose you're right. Well, we've been having this ongoing argument about . . . well . . . about sleeping together. He's very persistent, and, we've been going together for almost a year now, and he wants . . . well, you know men. He's been getting these fights going, and I wind up getting so mad that I just slam the phone down, or walk out of the room or something. I just find it very hard to argue with him. Every time I try to talk about how I feel about it in an intelligent manner, he starts getting mad. I know that it's awfully frustrating for him, but why can't he understand how I feel? Anyway, I can never argue with him. I just tighten up and get all upset, and I'm a wreck for the rest of the day. This morning, when he called, he said that he'd made reservations at a motel for us where we're going to spend the weekend, and I told him that he should've asked me first. Well, he got mad and started yelling, and I've been a wreck ever since. All I could do was slam the phone down. I couldn't talk, I couldn't yell—I couldn't do anything but get upset.

T.   I see. Do you get upset like this when you argue with anyone else, or just with him?

C.   I guess I'm just not a good arguer, or something. I could never argue against anybody. All I ever could do when someone got mad at me was to run away. So I guess it's not just him.

T.   Hmm, now do you get this same reaction when you argue about any topic, or is it just when the topic of sex comes up?

C.   Oh, it could be about anything, not just sex. I guess I just have no backbone. There's something else that I think might be important for me to tell you. Whenever I get into one of these arguments and get upset, I usually get very depressed afterwards. I don't know why that happens, but as I get less and less upset, I get more and more depressed. Does that make any sense?

T.   Can you describe these depressions for me?

C.   Well, I don't know. How can you describe a depressed feeling? I just get . . . depressed . . . I feel sad and lonely, and I can't get interested in anything. I just sort of mope around my apartment until it passes. I watch TV or try to read or something like that. Sometimes I call one of my friends and that makes me feel a little better. You know, it seems to me that sometimes, when I'm depressed, it's not just sadness that I feel. There's something else there too, but I can't seem to put my finger on it. I guess I'm pretty messed up, aren't I? I'll tell you one thing, though. I feel better now that I've told someone about it. It sort of makes me feel like I'm not so much alone anymore. Do you think I'll ever get over this?

T. I think you've made a pretty good start today. I'd like you to consider setting up appointments to come in and talk about the difficulties you've been experiencing. How do you feel about that?

C. Well, very truthfully, I was afraid you'd say that. I guess I'm afraid that there may be something really wrong with me. But, if there is, I guess it's better to try and get rid of it now than to let it go on, and maybe get worse. I guess that if I can figure out why this happens to me, I'll be able to figure out some way of coping with it.

Although Miss A.'s approach to therapy still reflects the fear and embarrassment experienced by virtually every client, it reveals her acknowledgment that the burden of discovering and understanding the reasons for her difficulties is her own. More important, her approach reveals that she is aware of the fact that understanding her problems is not enough. When she does come to such an understanding, she must then find ways to change, or, as she put it, to "cope" with the situation. She makes few demands of the therapist or of the therapy situation. In this respect, she is quite realistic.

It is important to note that not everyone will begin to feel better as quickly as Miss A. has. Therapy is in no way a continuously pleasant experience. Certainly, one who must reveal the most painful aspects of his life to himself and to another will not always feel good about it. The process of therapy involves considerable anxiety and discomfort for most people, and this aspect of therapy must be kept in mind by individuals who expect to feel better immediately.

The next excerpt involves a thirty-five-year-old middle-class man who holds a fairly well paying middle-management position. He is married and has three children. He was very reluctant to enter psychotherapy, arguing that he didn't need it and that "there are many people in the world who are really sick, so why should I waste the therapist's time?" The following is an excerpt from his first interview.

Therapist. Well, Mr. B., perhaps you can tell me a little about what brings you here.

Client (hesitant and anxious). I'm really not sure. My wife has been after me to come, but I really don't think I should be here. There really isn't anything wrong with me. I . . . I really feel like I'm wasting your time. . . . You should be spending your time with people who really need help.

T. I see, your wife has been after you to come in? Why does she think you should be seeing a psychotherapist?

C. Oh, she says that . . . well . . . I don't really know why. She just has been after me to come in, that's all. Maybe she's the one who should be here—not me.

T. Sounds like you're kind of mad at her for pushing you into this.

C. Yeah. I don't really think there's anything wrong. As a matter of fact, I bet she never thought I'd actually do it (laughs).

T. It sounds to me like you've come in more to get your wife off of your back than for any other reason.

C. You know, that just may be the truth. At least now I'll be able to shut her up when she starts in on me.

T. You know, we haven't talked at all about you—just your wife.

C. Yeah, I guess you're right. Well, maybe I should talk about me then, huh? Well, what do you want to know about me? . . . (Laughs.) I guess you'd probably want to know why my wife wants me to come in, right? I mean, that's what you asked me before, right? Well, you see, we . . . we haven't been getting along too well lately. Actually, it's more than just lately. We haven't been getting along well for some time now. I just can't figure out what it is. I've been getting moody. I guess it's the pressure from the job, and from the kids and all, and she gets moody too, and we get on each other's nerves. You know how it is, don't you, I mean, I suppose it hapens with lots of people. Anyway, I'm sure it's just a passing thing, and as soon as we have a good vacation, things will settle down. We haven't taken a vacation in a couple of years. Well, I'm sure it'll all pass. It's not very serious.

T.   It sounds like you're really fighting hard to believe that it's not serious, and that it will pass soon. I wonder if you're really afraid that it is serious, and that it might not pass so soon.

C.   It's just that I don't understand why I'm so moody. I mean, everybody has pressures. Everybody has a family that they have to support. Why has it affected me this way and not everybody else?

T.   You're afraid that there's something really different about you.

C.   Yeah. I get the feeling that . . . well, sometimes I think there's something really wrong with me, and I don't know what it is. It's frightening . . . it's just so frightening. And I sit here like a dumb fool spilling this all to you. You're not me. How can you understand what my situation and my problems are like if you're not me? I guess I have to deal with this myself. I just don't see how anyone else could help.

T.   You sound pretty hopeless about it, like you might be afraid you're beyond help.

C.   It's just that I don't know how you could help. Not just you—anybody. I do feel that it's hopeless sometimes. I don't even know where to begin or how to start. I mean . . . well, how do you fix somebody's mind? I mean, do we just sit here and talk? That's what I've heard. But how does just talking help? I mean, how can my telling you what's going on help me change things?

T.   Perhaps by sharing your problems with me, you'll be able to get a clearer picture of what is making your life so difficult. It's very hard to keep fear and pain locked within yourself. Perhaps by letting it out, you'll be able to feel better about it. Sometimes the things we are most afraid of and most concerned about wind up being less painful than we think if we can talk about them.

Mr. B.'s interview illustrates the apprehension, fear, and despair so frequently seen in individuals who enter psychotherapy. Even without knowing what Mr. B.'s exact difficulties are, we can be sure that he is by no means unique. Rather, his fears about himself and his doubts about how psychotherapy works are quite common. Further, Mr. B's interview illustrates one of the main principles of psychotherapy—sharing and revealing some of the most personal and perhaps painful aspects of oneself to another person. This aspect of therapy will be discussed further in Chapter Three.

Another reaction to entering psychotherapy is illustrated by an interview with a thirty-year-old woman. Her reaction is also not unique. It reveals a very common misconception about psychotherapy: the belief that a therapist fixes or repairs the mind of the client. In part, this belief has grown out of the assumption that psychotherapy procedures parallel medical procedures. Typically, the person who is suffering from a physical illness goes to a physician, who repairs the damage. This is often done through the use of drugs and/or surgery. The psychotherapist, however, does not "fix" people the way a physician fixes bodies. Rather, in psychotherapy, the client must bear the burden of aiding himself. This is one of the reasons that therapy sometimes is hindered. The client goes to the psychotherapist and expects the therapist to "do something" that will make things better. The therapist is not a magician, and there is little magic to be found in therapy. He can offer only questions, encouragement, support, and understanding. He cannot say magic words that will change the world in which a person lives.

Neither is the therapist a superman. He cannot be asked to do the impossible. When a frightened client demands to know "am I really crazy? Is there any hope for me?" after the first five minutes of the first interview, the therapist cannot honestly answer yes or no since psychological difficulties are often difficult to assess and appraise.

We have the case of Mrs. C., who tries to overcome her fears of her situation in life by presenting them to the therapist, demanding to know what he thinks of her "mental condition," and begging that he cure her at once.

Client. Doctor, you have to help me. I don't know what's happening to me. I'm afraid I'm cracking up. Please do something!

Therapist. Tell me about what's happening.

C. I really don't know. All I know is that I keep getting these reactions from people like I'm crazy or something. I don't know why. Is there really something wrong with me, doctor?

T. People react to you like you're crazy?

C. Yes. First it was my husband, and then my friends, and now even my children. You've got to help me. I know that other people have gotten help by seeing someone. Can you prescribe something for me? I can't sleep at night, and I'm tired all day long. I just don't know what's going on with me.

T. Mrs. C. . . . try and calm down a little and explain things a little more.

C. I told you. I think I'm cracking up. Nobody listens to me. My husband, my friends, my children—they just ignore me. It gets me so mad I could just scream. I get all tense and nervous, and that just makes it worse. A friend of mine was seeing someone once . . . for . . . for problems . . . and she got some pills that helped her. Maybe there's something like that that I could take—something to calm me down a little, so I wouldn't get so nervous. There's got to be something you can do to help me.

T. Mrs. C., it's hard for me to try and help you until I have a clear picture of what the trouble is. You say that people have been ignoring you. Can you tell me more about that?

C. Well, it's like my opinions about things don't matter to anyone. They never take what I say seriously. I feel like a little child who's fighting to be recognized. It's like I don't count, like I don't matter. What's wrong with me, doctor? Am I really cracking up? I've been afraid of that for a long time now . . . of cracking up. I just don't know what to do anymore.

T. Can you tell me about how all this started, and what was going on in your life at the time? It's still hard to see clearly what has been happening.

C. What's the matter with you? I told you already that I'm tense and nervous, and that people act as if I'm unimportant. Isn't that enough? All I want you to do is prescribe something to make me better. Can't you do that? If I could calm down and sleep at night, I'm sure that that would help.

T. You know, you've been telling me two different things at once. First you say that you think that you're cracking up, and that you want help and then you say that the only thing that's wrong is that you can't sleep at night, and that you just want a pill for that. So I'm really not sure as to what you see as being the problem.

C. I guess the problem is that I'm a nervous person, basically. I'm nervous a lot of the time, and when I have to talk with people, I really get nervous, and when they don't pay any attention to me, it just gets worse, and then I brood about it and get mad, and then I can't sleep at night. Isn't there some kind of pill or something that will make me less nervous? I think that if I could just be calmer, all this wouldn't happen.

T. Well, it's true that there are some drugs—tranquilizers —that sometimes help people relax more, but . . .

C. (breaking in) Yes, that's it. That's what I want. Can you prescribe something like that for me?

T. It seems to me that it might be of more use to you if we could explore this nervousness. We might be able to find out what it is that makes you so nervous, and try to deal with that. That would seem a more productive approach in the long run than simply taking tranquilizers. How would you feel about that?

C. I don't know. I thought that I'd just come and see you, and tell you my problem, and that you'd give me something to help me. I didn't think about the other thing you just said. It sounds like you don't want to give me anything to help me. It sounds like you want me to do something else, but I don't understand what it is or how it could help me. Are you really trying to tell me that I am crazy, and that I'll have to come to see you for a long time? That's it, isn't it?

T. Look, Mrs. C. I can understand how upset you are. People who come to therapists are very upset and frightened just like you are. But simply being upset and frightened is not the same as being crazy. The word "crazy" doesn't mean very much to me. People can have problems in their lives which range from being trivial to very serious without being necessarily "crazy." As far as you are concerned, I haven't spoken with you enough to even get a clear picture of what your difficulties are, much less pin a label on them. As far as pills are concerned, I can certainly get them for you, but I'm not sure that you really would profit as much from them as you seem to believe. Pills are not cure-alls, Mrs. C. They may help a person feel better for a while, but they don't help us find out what is making the person upset in the first place. That's why I'm not sure that pills would be the best thing for you. I just don't have a clear understanding of the difficulties you are facing. What I would like you to consider would be to set up appointments with me, and try and discuss the problems you are having. Very often, if the problems are brought out into the open, the people who have them can get better ideas as to how to deal with them. All I can do is to be here to listen to you, and try to help you talk about what's bothering you. I can't do much more than that. You're the one who is going to have to do most of the work.

C. Well, you said that I should come back for more appointments. How long do you think it'll take?

T. I really couldn't begin to try to estimate that, Mrs. C. Sometimes it takes weeks, and sometimes years. It's very difficult to say. However, the length of time it takes isn't necessarily related to how serious the problems are. Sometimes more serious problems take no longer to deal with than less serious problems. But as to how long it will take for you, I'm afraid I can't answer that at this point in time.

Clearly, Mrs. C. has much to learn about therapy. She makes unrealistic demands on the therapist, expecting him to be able to tell her "what is wrong" and prescribe some drug to remove the problem, without being at all clear about what her problem really is. She must learn that the therapist is neither a mind-reader nor magician and that he does not "cure" people. In summary, it must be reemphasized that the burden of dealing with painful experiences lies with the client, not the therapist. The client's task is to talk—to reveal his fears and hopes, his shame and his pride, his successes and his failures. He must be as explicit as possible when dealing with his difficulties, for the therapist can only be of help when the client presents his thoughts, feelings, and actions in a clear fashion.

Explicitness helps the therapist clarify the client's thoughts and feelings. Further, the client helps the therapist identify those aspects of his life that make him fearful, anxious, or upset. The therapist is aided and the client sees and understands those aspects of his behavior that may lead him into difficulties.

It is important to note that rather than the therapist helping the client, it is the client who helps the therapist, and thus helps himself. Effective therapy cannot be accomplished without the client's complete involvement and maximum effort. To expect any beneficial effects from therapy without this effort would be unrealistic and foolish.

One final point concerning the way in which therapy works must be made. Inevitably, therapy involves some kind of change on the part of the client. This change may be a behavioral change. That is, the client may come to behave differently. The change may be in the way one views the world—a shift in perspective, perhaps. In any case, change is practically the most important aspect of therapy.

The old adage "You can lead a horse to water but you can't make him drink," is directly applicable to psychotherapy and the change that therapy involves. The therapist can point out possible changes and their probable consequences; only the client can accomplish the change.

Tremendous courage and strength must be mustered to make such a change. Those clients who are willing to help themselves generally fare better in therapy than those who expect the therapist either to change them or to change their world. Those who enter therapy expecting the world to change for them are least likely to reap the benefits of therapy. Often, such a person says he wishes he were different, or he wants to change; what he *means* is that he wishes the world would change. When he realizes that no one can change the world, he may become angry and convince himself that the therapist is incompetent. The client's unrealistic belief that someone can change the world is the real problem.

CHAPTER 2

The Psychotherapist:
What He'll Want to Know

The first meeting of two persons is usually marked by the passage of information between them. Each person wants to know certain things about the other so that he might form some impression or opinion. This applies in a doctor-patient relationship as well; however, specific types of information are passed back and forth and the burden of providing personal information rests with the patient.

Providing information that will enable a physician to diagnose physical illness is relatively simple. The physician asks about pain, abnormalities, difficulties in physical functioning, and so forth. Because a cultural model is available as a guide for the physician-patient relationship, the physician can obtain these facts rather easily; most patients are well-trained and more than willing to provide as much information as the physician needs.

The psychotherapist's area of concern is not so well-defined as the physician's. When a patient arrives at the psychotherapist's office, he is usually not aware of this fact and may initiate a conversation similar to the following:

Therapist. How do you do, Mr. D.? Won't you sit down and tell me why you've come to see me at this time?
Client. Well . . . It's kind of hard to figure out, Doc. . . . I was fine until about three months ago. Since then, I feel anxious most every day. It's real bad, too. I can't keep my mind on my job. I've been jumpy with my wife

and kids. I'm jumpy, just jumpy. I figured maybe I'd better see somebody about it, 'cause I just can't get over this tight feeling. What do you think I should do?

T.   You said you were fine until about three months ago. Did anything occur around that time which might have changed you or your life in any way?

C.   No . . . I can't really think of anything.

T.   Well, perhaps it's hard to think back that far and see if anything really affected you—we'll get into that later. You also said, though, that you feel anxious almost every day. Is it at any particular time of the day that you feel tense?

C.   Well . . . it's usually worse late at night after the kids have gone to bed. I just find that I sit down to relax after a hard day at work and I just can't get rid of the tension. My wife tries to talk to me and I get mad at her. She's kind of sensitive and gets hurt when I do this. I just can't help it; everything she says just seems to rub me the wrong way.

T.   You mentioned before that your children are also getting on your nerves. Can they say things to you without your getting angry at them?

C.   Come to think of it, doctor, it's usually only after I've had a spat with my wife that I really can't stand the kids around.

T.   So it seems that you really only become "jumpy" in response to your wife. I think that's kind of important. Have you been having any particular difficulties with your wife in recent months?

C.   (Pause.) We've been arguing a little more than usual, maybe . . . well, not really, I guess it's just about the same as it's always been.

T.   It seems that you're a little hesitant to say that things are bad at home—almost as if you'd rather not discuss conflicts with your wife.

C.   No, really, everything is fine between me and my wife.

T.   This might make you a little uncomfortable, but I'd like to ask you a few questions about your relationship with Mrs. D. Although you deny any difficulty with her, I strongly feel that there is some problem there. Perhaps it's a sexual one. (Silence. Patient is holding his head down.)

T. You seem to be quite anxious about this, but I really feel its important that we discuss it.

C. I know you're right . . . but . . . it's just that I really don't know what to do. (He appears to be becoming more emotional.)

T. About what, Mr. D.?

C. I'm afraid that I'm losing my wife.

T. What makes you think that?

C. She just has no interest in sex anymore and I think it's because there's someone else.

T. Because she seems to have lost interest in sex, you conclude that she's seeing another man. Doesn't seem like you've thought too much about this.

C. You're wrong. I've been able to think of nothing else for months.

T. Have you spoken to your wife about your feelings?

C. I just can't bring myself to ask her . . . if she says it's true, I don't know what I'd do.

T. So you go along living with the one person who can confirm or allay your fears and you don't ask her to tell you if you're right or wrong?

C. I just can't . . . I wish I could but I can't. If I found out it's true . . . you have to help me.

T. Mr. D., I think that there seems to be some breech of trust in your relationship with your wife and neither of you can talk to the other about it. Hopefully, this is something we can work out in psychotherapy.

The therapist has now spoken with the client at some length and has been able to define the problem that is upsetting his client more clearly. He has narrowed the client's complaint from vague jumpiness to a difficulty in his perception of his wife's fidelity, and is ready to search his client's background.

The therapist will ordinarily be interested in several major areas, including his client's childhood, education, social background, work and leisure-time activities, family status, etc.

A client's childhood is important, for many habits, attitudes, and coping techniques are learned during this period. The therapist can learn a great deal about a client, for example, by inquiring as to which parent the client feels most similar to or which parent was the client's favorite. In addition, certain incidents that occurred in childhood have lasting effects upon people. If the client remembers isolated events of his childhood, they usually have some special emotions attached to them and are worthy of further exploration.

Social background is perhaps most important. Since, often, a person seeking therapy is having difficulty relating to others in a comfortable manner, an investigation of social development can be most revealing. Information such as the client's adolescent dating experiences, age at first date, history of sexual contact, friendship patterns, and social successes and failures are often discussed. But the therapist must also know facts about the present. An in-depth discussion of all relevant aspects of the client's present life situations is necessary. Here, the therapist attempts to determine the extent of his client's problems. He sees whether the client's work, home life, sex life, and social life are affected. Next, he tries to determine the frequency and intensity of the difficulties so that he can formulate some explanation for his client's complaints.

It almost seems as if the questions will never stop, but the client must allow the therapist to know him as few other people do. He must reveal his hidden and tabooed thoughts and feelings. Such information about a client provides a basis that enables the therapist to see how and where his clients complaints fit into his life. The therapist wants to know when his client's problems started and how he has handled difficulties in the past. He wants to know this human being sitting across from him better than any other person the client has ever encountered. Unlike his medical counterpart, the psychotherapist cannot isolate a part (a hand, a foot) of an individual and treat it. The target is the person's entire essence—his being.

With this barrage of explanation, we will look at another sample interview.

Therapist.   Good afternoon, Miss E. I'm Dr. Mitchell. . . .

Won't you sit down? Why have you come in to see me this afternoon?

Client (visibly upset and wringing her hands in anguish). It's school, Doctor, it's . . . it's driving me crazy. Look at me . . . I . . . I just can't do the work. The professors are hard on me . . . I don't know why. I'm just too upset to do anything . . . I want to do well . . . why can't I?

T. Let me see . . . according to your record, you're in your second semester of your freshman year at Southeast College. When did you start having the difficulties you're describing to me?

C. I guess it was just after mid-term exams last semester.

T. Did anything happen then that might have something to do with your being upset?

C. Well, I don't know if this has a great deal to do with it, but my father really expects me to do well in college. I really blew my mid-term exams and he just hit the ceiling when my mid-term grades came home.

T. What do you mean when you say he hit the ceiling?

C. He started pulling his old routine of how he's working so hard to send me to school and how I'm not paying him back for his efforts . . . You know how it goes, I guess.

T. I'm afraid I really don't.

C. I just get so mad when I talk about it . . . I don't know what it is . . . I know what he's doing to me, but I still get all tied up inside when he starts yelling at me about letting him down.

T. After he started yelling at you about your grades, you began feeling the way you do now?

C. I think so.

T. You weren't quite sure about your father's reaction to your grades having a great deal to do with your problem. Was there anything else which occurred around that time?

C. Like what?

T. I don't really know, but I think there is something more going on than you say.

C. Will my father be able to find out anything that I say to you?

T. Only if *you* tell him.

C. If he ever finds out the reason why I flunked my exams, he'll just kill me.

T. It's something which would upset him even more than failing?

C. That's an understatement . . . well, I know I'm not going to tell him and you're not . . . it's probably important . . . My father, you know, is really hung up on my marrying well . . . he doesn't like it when I go out with boys who are not from "good families" . . . when I got to SC I met this boy, a junior . . . he was the nicest boy I ever met . . . he was nice to me and gave me things and made me feel secure . . . I was really excited about him and I told my mother about him. . . . Well, it wasn't long before my father called me and wanted to know the usual about him . . . you know, what does his father do, where does he come from, what's his religion. . . . My answers weren't good enough for him, I guess, and he told me he didn't want me to see Josh again. . . . For the first time in my life I told my father that he had no business telling me that and that I was going to keep on seeing Josh. Boy, did he blow up. . . . I stood my ground O.K., but I really felt terrible after I hung up the phone.

T. So this confrontation with your father really got you upset. What happened then?

C. (starting to weep). Well . . . just before mid-terms I was having lunch in the cafeteria and I heard some of Josh's friends talking about him and his girlfriend, me. They were . . . oh doctor, this hurt me so much . . .

T. I understand, Miss E., take your time.

C. . . . they were laughing about how Josh was having some trouble winning his bet . . . (crying) . . . he . . . he had a bet with them that he could pick out any girl in the freshman class and get her . . . get her to go to bed with him by the end of the semester . . . the freshman he picked was me . . . (sobbing).

T. I see how much this has upset you and its something we'll have to talk about again. If you can, though, I'd like you to tell me what happened after that.

C. I'll try . . . needless to say I wasn't really in the mood for studying for my exams, I just sat in my room and cried. . . . I didn't want to see or talk to anybody. . . .

The worst thing about it was that I didn't want my father to find out . . . I didn't want him to say, "I told you so."

T. What did you do about your father?

C. I didn't tell him. . . . I haven't told him.

T. You mean for six months you've been able to hide your breaking up with Josh from your father.

C. (crying again). Yes . . . I make up stories about the fun I'm having with him and I tell my father. I'm trying to show him that *I* was right about Josh, and that I'm old enough to not need him to pick my boyfriends.

T. That must be a very hard lie to live.

C. That's why I came to see you . . . I just can't get out of it. School is almost out for the summer . . . I can't go home . . . I just can't . . .

T. So, Miss E., you've gotten yourself into a dilemma. On the one hand, you want to forget Josh because of the way he hurt you and on the other, you don't want to let your father know that you made a mistake when you went against his advice. I think by talking this out clearly we may be able to arrive at some solution. Let's go back to your feelings about being used by Josh. . . .

The above interchange began with the client making a vague statement of her symptoms. She was hesitant to talk about her boyfriend because she was afraid that her father might discover what had happened. The policy of confidentiality described by the therapist set her mind at ease and made it easier for her to talk openly. Here, the therapist was trying to direct the client towards a statement of the problem as it really was; he was not willing to accept a partial explanation (mid-term failures). He was trying to find out about *all* of the pressures bearing upon his client's life at the time of symptom onset; he wanted to know more than that which the client initially felt sufficient to tell him. Were he not skilled in this task, the client would surely have suffered the consequences of his superficiality.

CHAPTER 3

"Opening Up": Overcoming Fear and Embarrassment

As we mentioned in Chapter 1, the client in psychotherapy must reveal and share with the therapist some of the most personal, private, and, often, painful aspects of his life. Our society, which values a person's ability to work out his own problems without burdening others and seems to foster alienation and poor communication, makes personal confidences difficult. In our cities, our suburbs, and our rural areas, people find it increasingly difficult to meet other people and to make friends. More and more, people keep to themselves and disapprove of the outgoing or friendly individual, who is regarded with suspicion and described as "pushy," "too friendly," or "nosey."

If a person approaches a stranger and tries to strike up a conversation, the stranger will usually become suspicious and frightened. But if these same people are introduced by a mutual friend, the response changes completely; they accept each other on trust. When a young man approaches a woman on the street or in a store, the girl may be cold and distant, and she may view his approach as an attempt to "pick her up." However, if the same girl were to receive a phone call from the young man as a result of a computer dating bureau, she might respond in a very different manner. No longer is he trying to "pick her up." Rather, he is being "introduced."

Another example of the type of relationship fostered by society may be seen in the case of "the new neighbor." More often than not, the new neighbor does not feel comfortable in his new surroundings unless either he or his neighbors make an unusually strong effort to welcome him. Frequently, it takes weeks or months of observation and evaluation before he becomes "established" in his new neighborhood. Throughout this period, he receives suspicious glances, perhaps some uncomfortable smiles, and even some "light" conversation. Rarely, however, do his neighbors greet him warmly and offer the comfort of friendly relationships. It may take months to establish close relationships and, sometimes, they cannot be established at all.

In a great many instances, relationships within a family are as strained, if not more so, as relationships between neighbors. Too frequently, a husband may be so wrapped up in his work that he is unable to respond to his wife when she is upset about something. Again too frequently, a wife may become so left out of the lives of her husband and children that she is unable to respond to their problems and their needs. Children often speak of the "communication gap" between themselves and their parents. In his own way, each family member may feel misunderstood and left out of the lives of the rest of the family at times.

It is important to note that children learn how to be adults by watching other adults. Since adults—primarily parents—serve as the models or leaders for their children, a child often gets the impression that to behave as an adult, he must keep to himself and respond to other people only when he must. As a result, the isolation so prevalent in our society is perpetuated. Other children may feel that there is a better way to behave, but if they have not been exposed to other behavior, they may become confused and lost in their attempt to find the better way. Frequently, they find it difficult to respond in a warm, trusting fashion, and the feeling of being isolated and alone is heightened.

In such a social environment, the individual who enters psychotherapy finds it difficult to open up, to reveal himself to the therapist. Opening up seems in many ways to be absolutely alien to the behavior he has learned. Thus, for many people, the fears of being found out and all the other fears about psychotherapy that were mentioned in Chapter 1 are compounded by how they have learned to relate to others. As a result, the major task of the psychotherapy client is also the most difficult.

By now the reader is probably aware that the crucial issue is really one of trust. The success or failure of psychotherapy is often the direct result of establishing, or failing to establish, mutual trust. It is, perhaps, the most important aspect of psychotherapy—and the most difficult to achieve and maintain.

In our society, trust is often held up as one of the most important values. We are taught in childhood that the capacity to trust is one of the most cherished and highly regarded aspects of human experience. However, we often find, through sad experience, that trust is frequently preached, but rarely practiced. We find that putting our trust in another often furnishes ammunition that can be used against us in moments of anger. We find that putting our trust in another makes it easier for the person we trust to hurt us should he desire to do so. In short, we learn that to trust another is to invite pain—that, although people tell us to act in one manner, they themselves act in another.

An individual who has been open and trusting and has paid the price in pain and hurt or seen this happen to others may find it very difficult to believe that there are people who can be trusted. He begins to see everyone as potential enemies and refuses to risk being hurt by being open.

If this is true of most people, it is especially true of the individual who enters psychotherapy, for it is more than likely that he has experienced a great deal of pain in his relationships with others. Thus, the person in psychotherapy must overcome one of the most basic, pervasive fears known to man and invest his trust in the psychotherapist.

Many times, the client himself is unaware that he is finding it difficult to trust the therapist. Sometimes, when a client finds it difficult to talk about some painful aspect of his life, the reason may be that he is afraid of revealing too much of himself to the therapist. An example of such a situation will now be presented in the form of an excerpt from the fourteenth therapy interview of a twenty-four-year-old male.

Therapist. You seem to be having some trouble talking about your relationship with your girl.

Client. Yes, I am. But I don't know why. I guess I don't know the right words to express it. I mean, it's hard to put your feelings about a relationship into words. They're just feelings, you know . . . I mean words can't really express them well.

T. Yes, I know it's hard at times, but you've been pretty successful in the past when it came to describing your feelings. I wonder if there's something special about this particular relationship that makes it hard for you to talk about it?

C. Well, it's a special relationship, of course. It's different from any relationship that I've ever had, so maybe that's why it's hard for me to describe my feelings clearly. I don't know . . . it . . . it's not that the feelings are so vague, or anything. Oh, I don't know. Maybe it's just a bad day for me.

T. A bad day?

C. I'm just all confused, and I'm having trouble concentrating. Oh, hell. I'm just disgusted with myself.

T. Disgusted with yourself?

C. Yes. I know that I should be able to tell you about this relationship, but for some reason, I can't. I don't know why. It's stupid.

T. What do you think might happen if you did tell me?

C. I don't know. Why do you ask that?

T. Well, I just got the impression that you might be afraid to tell me for some reason, and I was wondering what that fear might be about.

C. (silence, 30 seconds). Well . . . yes. In a way, I guess I am a little frightened to tell you, but I'm really not sure why. There's sort of something inside me that's holding me back . . . it's like . . . well, it's just a feeling I have that I'd better not tell you. I can't explain it.

T. Tell me, these feelings you have about your girl, are they painful or upsetting to you?

C. Yes, they are.

T. Then perhaps one of the reasons you don't want to tell me is that you're afraid that I wouldn't understand.

C. No, I know you'd understand. You always have in the past. I don't think it's that . . . I don't know what it is . . . it . . . it's not like I don't trust you or anything . . . but . . . oh, I don't know. Really, I don't.

T. Well, maybe it's that you don't trust me. I know that you've been hurt many times when you did put your trust in someone. It must be very hard for you to trust most people, so I can understand that you might find it hard to trust me, too.

C. But I do trust you . . . at least I think I do. You know, I'm not even sure any more what it means to trust someone.

T. Well, maybe we can talk about that, since it seems to be an important area for you. What does trusting someone mean for you?

C. What does trusting someone mean? I wish you hadn't asked me that. I really don't know. It's been so long since I've trusted anyone . . . I can't even remember . . . well, I guess I trusted my mother. (Laughs.) What a joke. But I learned. I learned fast. It was a hard lesson, but I learned. You wouldn't believe the things she did to embarrass me. Every time I'd tell her something —anything that meant something to me, I'd have it thrown right back in my face. But I learned. After a while, I'd never tell her anything. (Laughs.) It was ridiculous! She once had the gall to ask me why I never confided in her any more. Can you believe it? That's what I call sick! Really sick! I guess that was the last time I ever trusted anybody. I mean, if you can't even trust your own mother, who can you trust?

T. Sounds like she really ruined your faith in humanity.

C. She sure did. Boy, I remember one time—I'll never forget it—I . . . I was . . . well, I used to have this problem with wetting my bed. I don't know why, but I had that problem for a long time. Do you know what she did? She waited until all her friends were at the house playing cards, and when I came in with a friend of mine and asked if he could sleep over at our house, she said, "Maybe your friend wouldn't be so anxious to sleep over if he knew that you still wet your bed." I was so ashamed . . . they all looked at me . . . all those women . . . and my friend . . . he just looked at me like I was a freak or something. I couldn't stand it. I ran upstairs and locked myself in my room, and I cried for hours. How could she do that to me? How could she? My own mother. The next day it was all over school. My "friend" had told everyone. Some friend! My mother and my friend. I didn't ever want to come out of my room again. I was so ashamed. I wanted to run away— to go somewhere where they'd never find me. They all kept teasing me about it. Kids are cruel that way, you know. They're merciless. And it was all my mother's fault. Later, when she came up and tried to come into my room, I wouldn't unlock the door. She said, "I did it for your own good, to help you stop." Can you believe it? For my own good! I'll never forgive her, never. She never could understand what she did to me. She kept saying how she'd done it out of love—to try and help me. Christ! If that was done out of love, it's a good thing she didn't hate me. Well, that was the last time she ever shamed me. I never gave her another chance. It was like I was a boarder in my own house. I didn't talk to her for about a month, and even after that, I never told her anything about me. That's when she started this "you don't confide in me any more" stuff. What a laugh. What a macabre joke!

T. It was a horrible experience. You must've been furious for a long time afterward.

C. You wouldn't believe how angry I've been. Like I said before, I'll never forgive her for that. I guess that's why I find it so hard to believe that it's OK to trust anyone. I guess that's why I was having trouble before telling you about what's been happening with my girl, too. Well, to tell you the truth, things haven't been going very well at all.

This young man's interview illustrates a very common situation. He has had such painful experiences as a result of trusting someone, that he finds it difficult to even conceive of trusting anyone again. However, until this situation was pointed out, he himself did not realize it. The more he can talk about his difficulties in trusting people, and the more he can share his fears of revealing too much of himself with the therapist, the more he can understand the experiences that have caused his inability to trust. However, he must realize that simply understanding his difficulties will not, in and of itself, make anything different or better. He can only do this for himself by investing more and more trust in the therapist. It is only through his active attempts to change that his life situation can improve.

Just as there are some individuals who are unaware of their inability to trust others, so are there some who are aware of this inability but have convinced themselves that no one can be trusted. Sometimes, such individuals become so strongly convinced of this that they cannot let themselves believe otherwise. To believe that there are no trustworthy individuals in the world makes trust society's problem, while to believe that trust is an individual experience makes the inability to trust the individual's problem. Thus, since many people would rather not think of themselves as having a problem, they cling tenaciously to the belief that no one can be trusted.

For such people, the experience of psychotherapy resembles a challenge. Therapy becomes an arena for a battle. On the one hand, the psychotherapist takes the position that he is truly interested in the welfare of the client. On the other hand, the client, who cannot easily accept the fact that anyone is truly interested in his welfare, may actually go so far as to attempt to catch the therapist betraying his trust so that his beliefs can be kept intact and he can continue to see the problem as society's. Such an attempt is illustrated in the following excerpt from the twenty-first interview with a thirty-three-year-old woman, Miss F.

Client.   You know something, I think I'm going to give up on men. I just don't think I'll ever find one that really cares about anyone but himself. Men are the most cruel, self-centered creatures on the face of this earth. I don't want to have anything to do with them anymore, I've had it.

Therapist.   What's happened to make you so angry and upset?

C.   Well, it's this last guy I've been seeing. He's just like all the rest. It's the last straw. I can't take it anymore. It's always the same thing. They tell you that they'll do anything for you, and then when you really want something, you might as well forget it. We just had a big fight. Oh, I don't really think I ever felt anything strongly for him, but when there's no one else, it's easy to think you care for someone. Anyway, I was beginning to like him a lot. He was always so nice to me, I mean he took me places and bought me things, and always treated me with kindness and respect, and I really started to think that this was going to be it. Boy, was I ever wrong. Isn't that the way it always is? Just when everything is going well, just when things are beautiful, that's when something happens to wreck things. It happens every time.

T.   You seem to be saying that every time you begin to get close to some man, something happens to break things up. Can you tell me more about what happened this time?

C.   Yes, well, things were just going beautifully, and I had this feeling that we were probably going to be serious soon, because we'd been seeing an awful lot of each other, and everything was right, I mean it was just great. Well, the other night, when we . . . well, when . . . we were sort of making love—you know, just hugging and kissing and stuff like that. Well, all of a sudden he started to get wise . . . with his hands, I mean. That's when I knew that he was just like all the others. That's all they're after. They don't care about anything else. Well, I got mad and told him to get out and never come back. It serves him right. He's just like all the rest.

T.   This same kind of thing has happened before, I take it.

C.   Sure. Every one of them, the same thing. That's all they ever really want. They're all alike. I knew that he wouldn't be any different, and I was right. It just took him a little longer than some of the others, but it came out—I was right all along.

T.   You say it took him longer than the others?

C.   Yes, we had been seeing each other for close to a year now, on and off. I've tried to do everything I could to please him, because he was always so nice to me. I wore the kinds of clothes he liked, and the perfume he liked, and everything. I've always been like that. I've tried to please just about every man I've ever known, but they always end up the same way—all the time.

T. What kinds of clothes did you wear to please him?

C. Well, you know what men like. Things with either scoop necks or plunging necklines, and real short skirts with that clingy kind of material, like this one I have on today.

T. Did you ever think of the possibility that the men in your life might've gotten the impression that you were being somewhat seductive?

C. Me? I'm not seductive. You're kidding. I just try to please them, that's all. They're the ones who have problems with seductiveness, not me. What are you implying? I don't think I like what you're saying at all.

T. Miss F, you are a very attractive woman, and I wonder if you are aware that men may easily misinterpret your efforts to please them, and think that you are really trying to be seductive?

C. I don't know whether to take all that as a compliment or a slam, doctor. I still get the impression that you think that I . . . well . . . that I sort of made them behave that way. Well, let me set you straight, doctor. I didn't make them behave that way at all. That's just the way men are, and you don't have to do anything to bring it out in them. They'll show their true colors after a while. All you have do is wait.

T. Are you waiting for me to show my true colors too?

C. Well . . . no . . . I mean . . . I don't understand you.

T. You've been saying that all men are alike, and that they're only interested in sex. I guess that since I'm a man, you probably think that's all I'm interested in too, and I suppose that you've been waiting for me to prove it to you.

C. That's unfair. I am not. Look, you're supposed to be helping me. Why are you torturing me like this?

T. I'm just trying to show you something about yourself. Tell me this: what would it take from a man to convince you that he was different from the rest, and that he wasn't just interested in sex?

C. Well . . . he'd have to . . . well . . . (silence, 40 seconds) . . . well, there's no way I can be convinced. After all these years, I know what men are. They've all been alike, and there's no way that anyone can make me believe otherwise.

T.   It seems to me that you've stacked the deck so that men can't win no matter what they do. You've decided beforehand that they can't pass the test, and then you make it impossible for them to pass it. Since they can't win, you can cling to your belief that they're all alike. And since I'm a man, I can only think that you've got the same kind of test all set up for me—a test which I couldn't possibly pass. Then, when I fail, you'll be even more positive about men. For instance, how did you feel before I told you that I thought you were attractive?

C.   Well, mad at you, I guess, but something else was there too, and I don't know what it was. I just felt something else, like . . . well, I sort of felt betrayed . . . like . . . I wanted to say, "Oh, not you too."

Miss F. has been confronted with a highly important aspect of the way she gets along with men. She believes that they are all interested in nothing but sex and tries to confirm her beliefs by acting and dressing in a seductive manner. When the men in her life respond in a normal way to her seductive manner, they have "proved" her right, giving her a convenient excuse to break off the relationships.

It will take some very trying therapy sessions for Miss F. to understand why she behaves as she does. More likely than not, she will try to make the therapist respond to her seductiveness so that she can continue to cling to her belief that men have a problem and she does not. It is important to note, however, that she may not be aware of planning or scheming to create such a situation. Rather, her behavior has become so much a part of her way of living that she repeats the performance almost automatically to rid herself of the discomfort she feels when involved in a close interpersonal relationship.

Further, as noted with respect to several of the individuals interviewed, simply understanding that she is uncomfortable in close relationships is not enough to help. She must use this understanding to help her change her response to such relationships. By telling the therapist that she felt betrayed by him, she has taken the first step; only by continuing to reveal herself in this manner will she be able to help herself.

Another aspect of opening up in therapy involves the expression of strong emotions or feelings. The society in which we live discourages the expression of strong emotions just as it fosters secretiveness and isolation. Individuals who do express their feelings are often called emotional—a word that often carries strongly negative connotations, such as "weak," "childish," or "infantile." Thus, fairly strong social rules prohibit the adult from venting his feelings. Unfortunately, there are countless times in our lives when we experience strong feelings of one sort or another. Though society may approve of holding such feelings in, the consequences may be negative for the individual.

As a result of the tendency not to express emotion, psychotherapy often provides an opportunity for emotional release. In therapy, an adult who prizes his reputation for being "strong" can cry, scream, and yell without incurring the therapist's disapproval, providing the emotional outburst is genuine. However, since the trust that must be established before a person can reveal himself is not easily achieved, the capacity to let go in therapy may be greatly hindered.

An illustration of the expression of strong feelings can be seen in the following excerpt from a therapy interview with a fifty-five-year-old male whose nineteen-year-old son has been a source of difficulty.

Client. That no good kid. I should've let them lock him up. I should've let them put him away and throw away the key—let him rot forever, that God-damned kid. I should've had him taken away years ago. Then none of this would've happened.

Therapist. What's happened, Mr. G.? You're very upset.

C. Upset? Are you kidding? I could kill that kid in a minute and it wouldn't bother me for a second. I could carve him up into little slices and feed him to the fish. That would be the first good thing that had come out of him since the minute he was born. I hate him! I hate him! It's a good thing he's not here right now. I'd kill him this minute. I'd murder him.

T.　Mr. G., can you tell me what's happened?

C.　What's happened? I'll tell you what's happened. My son —my wonderful, beautiful son. The light in my life. My snot-nosed, dirty, rotten, punk of a kid just raped a girl. That's what happened. I knew that kid was going to turn out this way from the minute he was born. (Screaming.) I could kill him! The bastard! That stupid rotten fucking little bastard! I could murder him! (Gets up and paces back and forth across the room, pounding his fist into his hand.) I don't know anymore. I just don't know what to do. That kid has been rotten since he was spewed out of his mother's rotten belly! I know, I know what all you people say—that it's the parents' fault. Everything is the parents' fault, isn't that right? Well, that may be true, but for this kid it's just one parent's fault—his mother's. She's done this to him. She helped him all the way along. Always covering for him— always protecting him. "He's only a baby," she'd say, "he's only a baby. How can you punish a baby? He doesn't know what he's doing." That's what she'd say. She always had to protect him. I tell you, doctor. From the minute that bastard kid was born, I lost a wife and he gained one. He couldn't do any wrong. It was always "the baby" this or "the baby" that. She ruined him. She wouldn't let anybody else near him. Nobody else could touch him. He was all hers. I wish he were all hers now! I wish I never laid eyes on him! It was bound to happen. I told her over and over again. I told her that she was ruining that kid. But no, she had to have her way. I never even mattered anymore. It was like all she ever wanted me for was stud service—so I could father her a son that she could take and mold into this, this . . . thing that passes for a human being. I'm not a jealous man, doctor. I tried my best not to be jealous over him— imagine, being jealous over your own son! Well, it was no good. I tried to tell her. I tried to let her know that she was treating him more like a lover than a son. That she was substituting him for me. She laughed, the bitch! She just laughed. I begged, I pleaded, but it didn't do any good. She had him and that's all she ever cared about. Stud service and a weekly check, that's me. That's all I ever was. Just stud service and a weekly check. I could kill them both right now! I just don't know what to do or where to turn anymore. I feel empty now, like there's nothing left inside me, just like an empty shell . . . (silence, one minute) . . . (beginning to cry) I'm not even angry anymore—I'm just empty and lost. What can I do, doctor? What can I do now? My life is wasted—it's meaningless. I have nothing—no one to share with, no one to be with even. There's just nothing to live for anymore. I just don't know where to turn. (Crying.) Why . . . why don't I just . . . why don't I just kill myself . . . and get it over with? I've been dying a slow death for almost twenty years now. Why don't I just hang it up now? I'm finished. There's nothing left to do. I'm too old to start again, and I . . . I've just had it. I just don't even want to live anymore.

T. It's tough to see any future at a time like this.

C. Future? The word doesn't mean anything to me now. There was a time, a long time ago . . . (crying) . . . I had a future then. Not now—it's all over now. There's nothing to look forward to. My wife . . . I suppose she's down at the lawyer's office trying to find some way to get him off. God know's where the kid is. Future? No, doctor, I can't see a future for me. Why don't you just let me go and get it over with?

T. Let you go? I wasn't aware that I was holding you.

C. (Silence, 40 seconds). No, you haven't been holding me, have you. You know, could it be . . . well, you know, I felt that . . . not that you were holding me, but like . . . well, like I was holding myself here . . . like you wanted me to stay—not because you were afraid I'd kill myself or someone else, but because you were really concerned about me . . . for me . . . oh, I can't explain it. It's just that it felt good to be able to let all that shit out of me. It's been building up for all these years, and I never broke down like that before. I don't know what got into me. I guess it built up so much . . . and now with what happened with the kid . . . I guess I couldn't bear it anymore.

T. That's nothing to be ashamed of, Mr. G. We all have

only so much that we can bear, and then we have to let it out somehow. It would be much better if we could let a little out each time we feel it, rather than holding it in until we can't stand it anymore.

Mr. G. has been able to let his hair down in front of his therapist and has come through the experience with a different outlook. During this particular therapy session, Mr. G. realized that the therapist was on his side and that he felt better when he could be completely open. He had the feeling that the therapist was concerned about him—not in a protective, paternalistic sense, but in the sense that the therapist appreciated him and his problems—and that because of this concern and appreciation, the therapist could accept the client's expressions without sitting in judgment.

Another form of emotional expression that often emerges in therapy involves the feelings that the client experiences with regard to the therapist himself. These feelings are almost always very strong and may be either positive or negative. Regardless of the nature of such feelings, they must be shared with the therapist, for they may be very helpful in revealing the ways in which the client relates to other people in his world. However, the individual who is able to tell another exactly what he thinks and feels about him is rare in our society. Thus, it is often most difficult for the client to reveal his feelings about the therapist. Since this aspect of therapy is so very important, an entire chapter (Chapter Twelve) has been devoted to it. For the present, we need consider but one more interview, which further serves to illustrate the ways in which a client can open up in therapy. The following has been excerpted from an interview with an eighteen-year-old girl, whom we shall call Susan:

Client.   I don't know why I keep coming here. Nothing has changed much since I started. I don't think that anything's going to change, either. There really isn't very much hope—not for me, and not for this world, either. Everybody is so wrapped up in their own little lives that they can't see the forest for the trees. They just don't see how miserable they all are. Nothing's changed, and nothing will change.

Therapist. What kinds of changes have you had in mind?

C. I really don't know. I just thought, at one time, that things could be different. But now I really see how rotten and miserable this world really is. What's really pathetic is that so many people live their inconsequential little lives and never realize how stupid it all is. They think they're happy, but they're really not, and they don't even know it.

T. Aren't you really saying that you feel that you are inconsequential, and that you're unhappy, and that you don't like the life you are leading?

C. Well, I don't know . . . I guess in some ways that's true, but at least I'm more honest with myself than most of the people in the world. They won't even look at themselves to see how miserable they are.

T. You know, I get the feeling that what you're telling me is a wish that everyone could be as miserable as you are. Do you think that might be so?

C. (One-minute silence) I . . . well, they are as miserable as I am, only they refuse to see it. They wear blinders all the time, so that they won't be able to see how inherently rotten the world is.

T. You mean that their blinders keep them from seeing how unhappy you are.

C. God damn it, why do you have to keep changing around what I'm saying. You want me to believe that the world is great and that everyone else is really happy except me, is that right?

T. It just seems to me that you're fighting awfully hard to keep this the world's problem instead of yours.

C. Well, it is the world's problem. Look, I didn't ask to be born. I had no choice in the matter at all. All of a sudden, here I am in this rotten place, and you tell me that I'm the one with the problem.

T. What I'm saying is that it's easier for you to see the world as being inherently rotten and meaningless than it is for you to say that your own life is unhappy. It's easier to say that you're right and the world's wrong, because this way you are relieved of the responsibility of doing something to change your life so that it becomes happy. You've made it the world's responsibility.

C.　I don't think you understand me very well, or you wouldn't be saying these things.

T.　It may just be that you don't understand yourself too well. I admit that there's plenty of grief, misery and unhappiness in the world, but I'm not sure that it's because the world is inherently that way. It seems to me that the world is pretty much what we make it, and I don't think that at this time in your life, you're prepared to fight hard enough to change things for yourself. It's easier to sit back and say that it's the world's fault. Now, instead of telling me what's the matter with the world, why don't you try and tell me what's the matter with Susan?

C.　Susan? What is Susan? Who is Susan? "Susan" is just a word—a name, but there is something deeper than just "Susan."

T.　Deeper?

C.　Yes, deeper. There's an essence, an entity that is much more basic than just "Susan." (Starting to cry.) It's no good—like an evil thing. I don't understand it, but I'm afraid of it. It's a frightening thing, and it's eating me up alive. I don't know how much longer I can stand it. It's nameless and faceless, and it hides down in the depths of me, always lurking, always there, as if it were waiting to come out, and it's evil and malevolent. I want to hurt it. I want to hurt it. I want to destroy it. (Breaking down and crying bitterly.) Oh, please, please help me get rid of it. I can't stand it. Please help me. I don't know what to do. All I know is that I don't want to be this way, but I can't help it. All that stuff I was saying about the world before—you were right. I just feel so all alone, like nobody could possibly understand me, like I'm left to fight it out on my own, and I don't even know what it is I'm fighting. And I resent anybody who doesn't have to go through this because they can't understand what it's like.

T.　What is there about yourself that's so horrible that it makes you hate yourself so much?

C.　I don't know. I keep thinking of things I've done, or things I've thought of doing— things which might be evil enough to make me feel this way. But I can't think of anything. I really can't. Oh, the usual stuff, of course, like having fights with my sister, and having temper tantrums, and running away from home, and stuff like that, but I really can't think of what it might be that's so terrible that I'm frightened of it.

T. Well, sometimes there may not be one terrible thing or experience. The way a person feels about himself may be the result of many life experiences, so it may be fruitless to try and find the so-called "traumatic" experience in your life.

C. Is that true? I thought that there must have been something that I did or that happened to me that made me like this, and that if I could figure out what it was, maybe I could understand it.

T. Not necessarily. It seems to me that the most important thing for you right now is to recognize the ways in which you behave that reflect the way you feel about yourself and to recognize how this affects your relationships. Once you can do this, you can find ways to change so that the nature of your relationships can change. You may find that one of the reasons you feel so alone is because you won't let anyone else in. By telling them that they all are stupid because they can't see how miserable they are, you may have driven them away, with the result being that you feel disliked and isolated.

    If Susan can view herself and her life in the world with others in a different light, it is probable that she will find a new way to behave. As the therapist has put it, this process begins by "letting someone else in"—opening up and risking pain from others in order to experience warm and endearing personal relationships. The therapist is the first person that Susan has let in. Once she is able to reveal herself to him and realizes that he will not hurt her for being so open, she will be able to try being more open with others. Such a change will take tremendous effort on her part—an effort that she will find well worth while.

    Now that we have examined the task of the client in psychotherapy, let us turn to some specific kinds of difficulties experienced by many individuals and examine the ways in which several have dealt with them. First, we will look at some of the problems that arise in relation to the family.

CHAPTER 4

Family Problems

Frequently, the actual psychological difficulties that a client experiences in presenting himself to a psychotherapist are not a result of his inability to cope or his unique maladjusted life style. At times, presenting himself for help can be seen as an admission of the client's failure to cope within his immediate family unit. This situation is often the case in the treatment of children. For example, parents may find that their child is constantly throwing tantrums, crying at the slightest frustration, withdrawing from friends, and so forth. They may report this to their pediatrician who, after having cleared the child physically, will probably refer the child for psychological evaluation and treatment.

Although, ostensibly, the child would be the client, the psychotherapist would more than likely include in his evaluations interviews with the parents alone, and with the parents and child together. If, at this point, the therapist feels that other siblings may be involved in the difficulties presented by the client, the entire family may be asked to appear.

During these interviews, the therapist will try to determine and evaluate the extent of the child's problem and to hypothesize the source of the problem. For example, in a child who is manifesting extreme moodiness, withdrawal, and temper tantrums, the therapist might find that there has been some difficulty in the child's behavior since his younger brother has reached an age at which he demands attention and privileges, such as storybook reading and helping with cooking, that were usually reserved for the "client." Of course, this would provide an obvious answer to the child's problems and simple counseling and advice from the psychotherapist might be sufficient treatment for the difficulty in the family.

However, there are often more subtle maladjustments, and although the psychotherapist may feel that the individual's problem is actually family-oriented, he may not be able to assess this accurately in one or two interviews. In a situation such as this, a program of family therapy may be undertaken, with the goal being further illumination of the family's capabilities to function adequately.

The following is a transcript of an early family therapy session. The family involved was composed of Mr. H., age 48, a laundry worker; his wife, age 47, housewife; and their two sons, Jeff, age 15, and Ron, age 14. Although the H.'s had two older children, both were married and no longer a part of the immediate family unit. Ron, the younger son, was originally referred as the "client." He was intellectually very limited and stood 4″ taller than his older brother, Jeff. Jeff was rather effeminate in his manner and bantered with Ron a great deal. Mr. H. was very loud-spoken whereas his wife was quiet and tended to keep to herself.

At the beginning of the first session, the therapist explained to the H.'s that the problems that Ron had been having appeared to be the result of difficulties in the family as a whole; he stated that this was the reason that all of them were being seen instead of just Ron. The following is what transpired during this session.

Therapist.   Well, does anyone have anything they'd like to say to start things off?

Jeff.   Yeh, it's all my father's fault (laughs).

T.   Why do you say that Jeff? (Jeff does not respond, but turns to his brother and both begin to giggle.)

Mr. H.   Come on Jeff, the doctor asked you a question. Why do you think it's all my fault? Tell him, Jeff.

Jeff.   I was just kidding around.

T.   You know, Jeff, even though you're laughing and saying that you were just kidding, I think you really meant what you said.

Jeff. Well, I didn't.

T. Ron, you've been laughing along with Jeff . . . Do you think that your father is the one who's at fault?

Ron. Well, he yells a lot.

T. About what?

Ron. Everything.

Jeff. Yeh, everything.

Mr. H. Both you boys know that the reason I talk so loud is that it's damn hard to hear anything with your record player on so loud. A man's got to talk loud or he won't be heard. Why do you have to play the records so loud, Jeff?

Jeff. They're made that way. When they record a song they record it loud. No matter how low you turn the volume, it's still loud . . . that's the way teenagers like it.

Mr. H. Come on Jeff, you don't think I'm going to believe that.

Jeff. It's true.

T. It sounds a little hard to believe, Jeff.

Jeff. You're just like the rest of them . . . you always pick on us teenagers.

T. It seems that you're claiming we're picking on you as a teenager instead of dealing with the fact that your father thought you were lying to him as an individual.

Jeff. I'm not saying another word. (He sits back and smiles.)

Mr. H. You see what I mean? You can't trust that boy as far as you can throw him. I've tried everything to teach these kids to be honest and responsible, but they never listen.

Mrs. H. If you'd stop yelling all the time, maybe they'd listen.

T. Mrs. H., the yelling really seems to bother you.

Mrs. H. Twenty-six years, I've been listening to him yelling about everything. He makes me nervous . . . he's gonna drive me outa my mind.

Mr. H. Oh, you know it just bothers you because of the headaches you've been having the last couple of years.

T. Headaches?

Mrs. H. Oh, well, they just started a few years back. I went to the doctor and he said they were from tension or something . . . he gave me some pills for them, but they make me so sleepy I can't do my work. I guess I've just learned to live with them.

T.   Does that mean that you've also learned to live with your husband's yelling?

Mrs. H.   It's not really the yelling that I mind so much as the name calling. A father shouldn't speak to his sons the way my husband does.

T.   What kind of name calling goes on, Ron?

Ron.   He calls us stupid and stuff like that.

Jeff.   Yeh, and he curses at us too . . . like he calls us useless bastards.

T.   Mr. H.?

Mr. H.   You know, doc, a man wants his sons to grow up to be men like he is. I try to take these boys fishing and hunting and they don't want to go. Isn't that right, Jeff? . . . Isn't it, Jeff? What do I get? Ron is so slow he doesn't even understand what I'm saying half the time. And Jeff is more like a girl than a boy. (Jeff and Ron look at each other and giggle.)

T.   How does it make you feel when your father talks about you like that?

Jeff.   I don't even listen to him anymore. He's always calling us names like that.

T.   Ron?

Ron.   That's right, but we call him names too.

Mr. H.   You boys really hate me, don't you? (Jeff and Ron remain silent, but look at each other and smile.) I asked you a question. You hate me, don't you?

T.   Mr. H., it seems that you keep demanding answers from your sons which are designed to get them into a difficult situation with you.

Mr. H.   If you don't keep after them, they just ignore you.

This session continued fruitlessly for about one-half hour more. The following is a transcript of what occurred a few sessions later.

T.   Well, how have things been going during the past week?

Mr. H.   No change, doctor, Jeff and Ron still won't listen and that damn record player is still loud as ever.

Jeff.   I turned it down, for heaven's sake.

Mr. H. Don't give me that, Jeff, you know it's still so loud I can't hear the TV.

Mrs. H. Why don't you move the record player, Jeff? It wouldn't be so loud in the living room if you put it by the window in your room.

Jeff. I can't do that cause the draft from the window would cause the tubes to crack.

Mr. H. Jeff, you don't expect me to believe that.

Jeff. There you go again, picking on me cause I'm a teenager.

T. Jeff, I don't see how your being a teenager has anything to do with what your father said.

Jeff. OK, you're all against me. I'm going to shut up again. I try to make conversation and look what I get.

T. I get the feeling, Jeff, that you think you're the only one in the family with brains enough to get anything done.

Jeff. I'm not talking.

Mrs. H. Why don't we talk about the ten dollars that's missing from my purse?

T. What about that, Mrs. H.?

Mrs. H. Well, we just about have enough money to live as it is, and yesterday morning I found my wallet ten dollars short.

Jeff. Don't look at me. I didn't take it.

T. Nobody had said you took it, Jeff. Why were you so fast to deny your guilt?

Jeff. Cause I know that they're going to blame me.

Mr. H. Why shouldn't we blame you, Jeff? Didn't you come home yesterday after school with two cartons of cigarettes? Where did you get the money to buy them?

Jeff. I told you . . . I found them.

Mr. H. Come on, Jeff.

Jeff. It's true. My friends and I were looking in garbage cans and found them.

Mr. H. Who's going to throw away two cartons of cigarettes, when they cost about four dollars apiece?

Jeff. There was this guy, he was throwing away a whole case of cigarettes. We asked him if he wanted them and he said that he was leaving town and didn't need them anymore. So we took a couple of cartons each.

Mr. H. Jeff, you're talking about somebody throwing out over a hundred dollars worth of cigarettes.

Jeff.   It's all true.

T.   Even I find that hard to believe, Jeff.

Jeff.   Nobody believes me. Well, I don't care. (He is now visibly angry and sits back in his chair and sulks.)

T.   Does this sort of cross-examination happen often in your home?

Mrs. H.   It never stops. I'm not saying that anybody's right, though. Jeff lies so much you never know what to believe, but my husband never stops asking questions until he's got these boys in tears.

Mr. H.   I've got to teach them responsibility. How are they going to get along as adults if they lie and steal? I work damn hard to feed and clothe this family.

Jeff.   Here it comes.

Ron.   Yeah, here it comes.

T.   Here what comes?

Jeff.   Dad's "I work hard" lecture.

Mr. H.   Well, it's true, a man should earn some respect for breaking his back for his family.

T.   But apparently, every time you try to tell the family you deserve respect for what you are doing, you lose even more.

Jeff.   Yeah, so why don't you stop telling us?

T.   Jeff, I noticed how quickly you joined me in what you probably see as an attack on your father. You never attack him in a serious manner, but when I did, you got pretty excited.

Jeff.   I was just agreeing with your point.

Obviously, the difficulties the family is experiencing are quite complex. Through the interviews, it became apparent that Mr. H. was the focal point of the problem when the problem was looked at superficially. Further analysis, however, yielded the finding that Jeff, the older son, had no misgivings about boldly lying to his parents or the therapist and was trying to manipulate people for his own gain. He had very little insight into himself, however, and he was unable to see that the stories he was telling were very difficult to believe. Jeff had learned that his parents would become frustrated by his constant storytelling and by their inabilities to reason with him and would sooner or later let things drop.

During the session, when the therapist began to question the truthfulness of his statements, Jeff finally felt threatened and responded with anger. It was apparent that Jeff was a very angry young man but could not deal with his parents on an individual basis. He therefore chose to accuse his parents of hating all teenagers. Through this approach, he was able to feel a part of a group and did not have to face the fact that he, himself, was unable to please or relate to his father.

Ron, who was the original client, reacted quite differently during the sessions. He sat very quietly, smiled at times, and looked at his brother, but he never said anything unless he was responding to a question. Mr. H. rarely spoke directly to him, but seemed more concerned with Jeff and his battle with him. Thus, Ron was left out of the family unit for all intents and purposes. His silliness and withdrawal were, in part, a result of this status in the family. Although he was not an active participant in the family conflicts, the fact that he was still a child and was classed with Jeff made him respond to the attacks on Jeff with many of the same feelings as his brother. Unfortunately, Ron did not have the intelligence or manipulative skills to deal with his feelings directly.

Mrs. H., very quiet, like her son Ron, was also a victim of the family conflicts. However, she had learned to let her husband alone. Mr. H. was a very strong-minded person who felt that his sons were attacking him personally through their development. Jeff was effeminate and Ron was "dumb." To Mr. H., this meant that he had failed as a male figure for his children and that this failure would be noticed by other people. Since this notoriety as a father of weaklings was more than he could take, Mr. H. reacted as though his sons' behavior was designed just to hurt him. Thus, he responded by appealing to their guilt reactions. He said things like "I work and slave to feed and clothe you and what do I get?" When this approach did not work, Mr. H.'s anger came quickly to the surface; he called his sons names, struck them, and otherwise tortured them emotionally with unreasonable demands and constant cross-examination.

The H. family did not remain in therapy for many more

sessions. As a result of the family strain, Mrs. H. suffered a schizophrenic reaction and had to be hospitalized. As a result of her breakdown, Mr. H., Jeff, and Ron were thrown closer together out of mutual loss. One can only hope that they will remain close when Mrs. H. returns to the family unit.

"My Parents Just Don't Understand"

In this chapter, we will be concerned with the problems individuals experience with respect to their parents. There are few people who have not experienced some difficulties in dealing with their parents at some point in their lives. In fact, we often look to our parents and the role they have played in our lives as being a contributing factor to our problems.

As we mentioned in Chapter 3, parents serve as "models" for children. Children learn most about what it is like to be an adult in our society by observing and imitating the behaviors and attitudes of their parents. Since the values that parents teach their children may become a permanent part of their personalities, and constitute a major shaping force in their lives, the hero worship with which children regard their parents often leads to difficulties that may arise in the following manner: children are taught by their parents that it is good to be honest, trustworthy, sincere, and open with others. Since these values are espoused by parents, children believe that their parents themselves live in such a manner. However, they often find that this is not so. They may find that their heroes do not practice what they preach; that they want their children to "do as I say, not as I do."

When a child finally accepts the fact that his parents are "hypocrites," he is faced with the problem of what to do with his values, which he has learned from the parents he has worshipped. To further complicate matters, he begins to lose the sense of who and what he is in the world—a sense that is often called "identity." This is so because the child who worships his parents uses them as ideals. He sets them up as worthwhile goals for which to strive. He tries to emulate them as much as he can, for it is in such striving that he formulates an idea of who and what he is and who and what he will become when he grows older.

When he concludes that his parents are no longer representatives of the ideal, he begins to lose his conception of the ideal; thus, he begins to search for heroes who can serve as new models of attainment. In his search, he goes through a stage that is characterized by attempts to be like a series of individuals who hold prominent positions in society. These become his new heroes, and he goes from one to the other, continually searching for the one that suits him best. For the young boy, such heroes may include politicians, teachers, athletes, criminals, artists, or scientists. The "cheerleader" type, the "promiscuous" type, the "Queen Victoria" type, or the "career woman" type may become the young girl's ideal.

Not only are these changes in heroes drastic; they are also so rapid that an adolescent girl may dress in long sleeves and high collars on one day and in a very revealing outfit the next. With such a state of affairs, it becomes increasingly difficult for parents to keep up with the changes. Thus, a parent may respond to his "baseball role" when the child has already become a politician. As a result, the parent cannot understand the child and the child feels misunderstood. This problem is popularly referred to as the "communication gap." The parent may feel that the child is being directly antagonistic toward him, while the child may feel that the parent is "just plain stupid, rigid, and unwilling to listen."

It is important to reiterate that the values a child learns from his parents are relatively permanent and constitute a major shaping force in the child's personality. In this respect, it must be clarified that the child who is seeking new heroes is not seeking new values as well. Rather, he is seeking people who live by the values he has learned. Thus, he

seeks heroes who are honest, trustworthy, sincere, and open
—not heroes who *say* that they live in such a manner.

Two new values emerge from the search for new heroes
with old values: integrity and consistency. These values become so strong that they supersede many of the old ones.
Thus, the child searches for a hero who is consistent in word
and deed—someone who practices what he preaches, regardless of whether he preaches the law of God or the violent
overthrow of the national government. The individual who
hurls invectives at policemen publicly as well as privately
has more integrity and consistency than an individual who
says that his boss is unfair but goes off to work each day
hoping to please that boss. Thus, the former becomes a hero,
while the latter is branded a "hypocrite."

Such an occurrence will now be illustrated by an excerpt
from an interview with an adolescent boy who entered psychotherapy after running away from home. He had not been
doing well in school, and his performance seemed to be related to poor motivation more than to a lack of intellectual
ability. "Tom" is telling the therapist about the conditions
that led to his flight from home.

Client. Well, it was mostly my parents. My parents just
don't understand how I feel, especially my father. God,
there's just no way that I can ever make it with him.
He's so rigid that I couldn't get him to reason even if
I wanted to, and I don't think I really want to any more.
It's just not worth the effort, and I don't think it would
do any good to try. I've just given up on him.

Therapist. You say that your parents don't understand how
you feel, Tom. Do you think you could tell me how you
feel. Maybe I can try and understand.

C. Well, like I said, it's mostly my father. My mother minds
her own business pretty much and stays out of both our
ways. It's my father who's really impossible. He's just
so rigid—so stuck in his ways. He just can't see that
there are other ways to live than the way he lives. He
can't see that there are other, more important things
than the things he thinks are important. He's always

on my back. He's always questioning me: did I go to school, who are my friends, what do I do when I go out at night? Man, you'd think I was a criminal or something the way he gives me the third degree. That's why I had to get out of there. I couldn't stand it any more. I had to take off and find out who I am. I'm sure of one thing. I could never be like him. Never. He's worked his whole life—he takes the bus every day so that my mother can have the car. He rides to work and reads his newspaper, just like a million other people, and they never look at each other or talk to each other. He probably rides that bus with the same people every day, but I bet he doesn't know any of them. I bet that none of them ever put the paper far enough down from in front of their eyes to see that there's a world out there, a world with other people. And he does this every stinking day of his life. He works all day, and then he comes home at the same time every day, and my mom gets dinner ready, and we all sit down to eat, and nobody says anything to anybody. We sit there in complete silence, unless he has something that he wants to scream at me for, like my hair or my friends or my report card or something. Then there's plenty of talking, but it's all from him. I've given up. I don't argue with him any more. I just let him rant and rave all he wants. It wouldn't do me any good anyway. He wouldn't listen even if I tried, so what's the use.

T. Tom, what are the things that you do that bother him? It seems that he's as frustrated as you are, and neither of you is willing to give an inch.

C. Give an inch? That's all I did for years. I'd sit there and tell him what was eating me, but he couldn't understand. He can't stand my hair long, and he can't stand it when I go out and he doesn't know where I am. You know, sometimes I go out with my buddies, and we just ride around and talk all night. We don't go anyplace special; we just get into the car and ride. So when I come home and he asks me where I've been, what can I tell him? He doesn't believe me anyway. Maybe one of these days I'll really do something and fulfill all of his great expectations.

T. It sounds like you really want to hurt him.

C. Hurt him? No, not really. I guess that I'm so frustrated that I don't know what to do anymore. I couldn't hurt him—not intentionally. Hell, he was everything I ever wanted to be until I was about ten or eleven years old. I just idolized him, and I used to pray that I'd grow up to be just like him. What a laugh. Now, he's the one person in the world that I'd never want to be like. He used to tell me stories about what it was like when he was a kid, and I'd listen by the hour—I could never get enough. When he came home from work, I'd run out to meet him. I was always so glad to see him again.

T. What happened to change things so drastically?

C. Well, I'm not sure. I guess that part of it was that I grew up a little and realized that he wasn't half as great as I thought he was. I found out that he had his faults, and I guess I found it hard to forgive him for that. I found out that he sometimes bet on the horses and sometimes he got drunk, and stuff like that. It used to drive my mother crazy half the time. And when he used to come home and tell us about what a bastard his boss was, and then he'd make sure that he never forgot the boss's birthday—always dipped into the savings to buy him a present. I couldn't understand it. As I got older, I realized that there was nothing special about him at all. In fact, the older I got, the more I realized what a nothing he was. I guess I got pretty disillusioned, and I started to wonder what the hell I was all about. That started early in high school. Other kids seemed to have some idea of what they wanted to be and what they wanted to do with their lives, but I never did. Oh, when I was little, I always wanted to do what my father did—be just like him. But as I got to know him—I mean really know him—I just lost the feeling of security that I always had as a kid. I guess I got pretty mixed up. Nothing seemed worth it anymore, and I couldn't get myself working, like in school. I just couldn't see any reason to work hard to do well, because I guess I was afraid that I'd end up like my father no matter what I did.

T. Tom, I think that it would be important for you to come to some decision as to what *you* think is important and worthwhile in life. Only after you come to some kind of conclusion about what is of value to you can you begin to work with some goal in mind. Perhaps we should start right there, then. What things in life are important to you?

At this point in therapy, Tom faces the difficult task of clarifying his values. This may involve breaking away from his home or finding a better way of getting along at home. In either case, he must first decide what is meaningful for him, and then begin to pursue his goals in life.

Many young married couples are confronted with another type of parental problem. They are in a middle position in life—a time of transition—that involves becoming independent of their parents and yet maintaining a close relationship with them. For many individuals, this is most difficult to do. They may feel that their parents are unwilling to give them up to their spouses or that they must now be extra careful not to exclude their parents from their lives, without sacrificing their privacy. Parents who understand this dilemma can be of great help, but when the parents are unaware of their children's mixed feelings, they may make the situation worse.

An excerpt from a therapy interview with Mrs. I., a twenty-one-year-old girl who has been married for one year, illustrates the situation. She is finding it difficult to tell her husband that she feels that they see too much of his parents.

Client. I'm so upset that I don't know what to do anymore. (Crying.) The situation has gone from bad to worse, and I don't know how to make him understand how I feel without hurting his feelings. He calls them at least three or four times a week, and they're over at our place at least once a week. It's not that I begrudge it to them. After all, he is their son. But why don't they understand that we need some time to be alone—some time to ourselves. My God, we hardly have any weekends without them. What can I do?

Therapist. It must be awfully frustrating to have them around so much.

C. Frustrating isn't the word. Oh, I'm so mixed up. I just don't know what to do. Every time I try to bring it up and talk about it with him, he gives this "don't you like my parents" stuff. I just can't make him understand that I do like them, but that I'd like them better if they'd leave us alone for a while. Everytime they come over, it's like a military inspection. They come in and ask what we've done with our place since they were last over. My God, what do they expect—new furniture every week? And then they ask whether I'm treating their son well. His mother starts in with the stuff about how drawn and tired he looks, and why don't I feed him more, and what has he been eating, until I just about flip my lid. What do they think he is—two weeks old? And of course I take all this personally. I've always had the feeling that they didn't want him to marry me. I could never understand why, and I've frankly given up trying. It's not worth it to me to beat my brains out trying to have something good for them to eat when they come, when all they say in the way of thanks is something like, "well, at least she has some idea of what a kitchen's for." They really know how to get to me. You should see what happens when we go on a vacation. They come over to officiate at the packing, to make sure everything we'll need gets packed. Then they want to know exactly where we'll be, how long we'll be there, and what route we're taking, "just in case." I wonder if their parents ever let them live their own lives. This is just crazy. I can't take much more of it. (Silence, 30 seconds.) I really shouldn't be so hard on my husband. He's really better than I make him out to be. I guess that he's so mixed up about it that he doesn't know what to do, either. Like, he's told me that he'd rather not have his folks over on a particular weekend, so that we could be alone. But then, they call, and he just can't refuse them. I know what he must be feeling. I'd feel the same way if it were my parents. You want to share things with them—after all, they are your parents. But you want to live your own life at the same time, and with parents like his it's hard to find that happy medium. I know that if we ever tried to tell them how we feel it would just insult them, and then my husband would never get over it, but we can't go on this way much longer—at least I can't. What can we do?

T. Mrs. I., do you have a picture of what the alternatives are at this point?

C. Well, it seems to me that we could either keep on like we're going, which I couldn't do. Or we could tell them how we feel, and risk alienating them completely. I don't think we'd really want to do that unless we had to. Other than that, I really don't know what to do.

T. It seems to me that there might be other ways to handle the situation. For example, you could tell them that you have other plans when they next ask to come over, and slowly fit them into your schedule less and less, until you reached the point at which you could get along comfortably. There are several ways, but I think that the first thing you have to do is talk to your husband about the problem. You seem to believe that he shares some of your mixed emotions about the situation. If he does, then you have to talk about it and try to come to some unified way of dealing with it. If he doesn't feel as you do, you will have to make him aware of how you feel and why, so that he will be able to see for himself what happens between his parents and you. Once you can talk about it with him, I'm sure that you'll come up with a solution. It's quite possible that what's really bothering you is that you can't communicate about it with him.

C. That may be true, but I'm not sure. At any rate, I guess I'll have to talk with him about it. I've lived with it myself too long already. It scares me to death, though—I mean how he might react.

T. He might feel that you're asking him to choose between you and his parents.

C. (Silence, 50 seconds.) (Crying.) Maybe. Oh, I just don't know what I'd do if he saw it that way.

T. Well, then. You have to make it clear to him that you're not asking him to make a choice, but it's important that you get this off your chest. He may not be aware of your fears at all, so it's best to try and tell him about them.

Mrs. I. really has more than one problem. She must find a way to deal with her in-laws and summon the inner strength to discuss the problem with her husband even though she fears that he will leave her when forced to decide between herself and his parents. It is likely that her primary fear is that she will lose her husband, but discussing her fears with both her husband and her therapist may help her find a solution.

Another problem area with regard to parents involves the double message. Double messages are characterized by overtly saying one thing while implying its opposite. The mother of the young man in Chapter 3, who embarrassed her son in front of others and then told him it was for his own good, exemplifies an individual who gives double messages. While she verbalizes a desire to help him, she also communicates a simultaneous desire to harm and embarrass him. Double messages, even when they are subtle, have a common effect. They make the person at whom they are aimed uncomfortable and make response difficult or impossible. Obviously, it is difficult to respond to two conflicting messages at once.

Double messages often reflect the mixed emotions that the sender feels about the receiver and, as such, are often used by parents with regard to their children. For example, it is not uncommon for a mother to want her child to succeed in life but to feel somewhat jealous when the child succeeds where she may have failed. Thus, a mother may tell her daughter that she is pleased with her daughter's choice of a husband, yet subtly communicate the feeling that she does not approve. A father may want his son to succeed at sports but forbid him to attend practice because of a made-up argument in the hope that the child will fail.

As noted above, the receiver of a double message is in a bind. He finds it difficult to interpret the message and is afraid to respond to one aspect of it because of the possibility that the response will heighten the sender's anger. Many children are familiar with the parent who, when angry, tells them "go ahead and do what you want. See if I care." The child knows that the parent is angry and feels reluctant to obey the overt message because it is only half of the real message. Failure to obey the overt message may result in a statement such as, "Well, what are you waiting for?" If the child responds to the overt part of the original message, he might next hear something such as, "you'd probably go ahead and do it no matter what I said." The situation smacks of being "dammed if you do and damned if you don't."

If such a relationship is maintained for a long period of time, the child may become frustrated and angry, as happened with the young man in Chapter 3. For a child, however, to break so completely with his parents is almost impossible. Parents hold a special position in our society—a position that gives them a great deal of power for a great deal of time. The following excerpt illustrates the case of an individual who has not yet been able to break away from his mother, who continuously bombards him with double messages. He is angry and frustrated, but he finds himself unable to take any action because of the fact that "she's my mother."

Client.   It gets so frustrating sometimes that all I can do is run up to my room and cry. I just don't know how to react to her anymore. If I do what she tells me she's mad at me, and if I don't do it, she's mad at me anyway. I just feel so trapped.

Therapist.   Can you give me an example of this kind of a situation?

C.   Well, let's see. The last time it happened was last night. I was supposed to go out with my girl, and I was getting ready to go when she came in and said something like, "It does my heart good to see you getting out so much. It's good for a boy your age to go out with girls. It's better for you than staying at home with your father and me." Now, what the hell was I supposed to say to that? If I'd said that she was right, and that it was better for me to go out than to stay home with her and dad, she would've gotten insulted. I could tell. And if I said she was wrong, and that I should really try to spend more time at home, she would've said one of two things. Either she would've said something like, "Why do you always have to disagree with what I say. Don't you think I have any brains at all?", or she would've said something like, "No, your dad and me, we'd just hold you back and cramp your style. It'd be best for you to leave us alone, even though you are our son, and we love you very much." Now, I ask you, is that fair? How can she do that to me? I mean, there's no way out. Either I insult her by agreeing with her, or I make her mad by disagreeing with her. I can't win. Like I said before, I'm trapped.

T. That must be a very frustrating feeling. What did you finally wind up doing?

C. Well, I thought about it for awhile, and I decided I'd better not go out, because I'd have to face my mother when I got back. I called my girl and told her that I couldn't make it, and then I told my mother that I wasn't feeling well enough to go out on a date, and that there was some work out in the back yard that I needed to get done. Then I went out and moped around in the back, and finally did the work. Then I went up to my room and stayed there until I went to sleep. I'll tell you, though, I felt pretty crummy about the whole thing.

T. So you got out of the bind by neither agreeing nor disagreeing with her, but by doing something that was sort of neutral or irrelevant.

C. That's about the size of it, although I never thought about it like that before. But that was lucky. I don't always manage to pull it off so well. I can't always come up with a way to get me out of the bind, and I wind up in an argument with my mother, and then I wind up feeling rotten about it. Sometimes I'd really like to tell her off. I'd like to tell her what she's doing to me, but she wouldn't understand, or she wouldn't want to understand. She'd just get all hurt, and call me a no-good ungrateful son who has no respect for his mother and that would really do it. Then I'd feel rotten for a week. I just know it would happen, because it's happened already—more times than I'd care to count. I just can't get out of it. It's impossible. I'd like to grab her and shake her and scream at her, and let her know what she's doing. (Silence, 30 seconds.) I couldn't do that, of course. Then I think that it'd be great if I could get out—move out to a place of my own. But I can't afford it, and even if I could it'd be impossible to do without destroying my mother. I mean, in spite of all of the crap she hands me, she's still my mother. I mean how can you hurt your own mother? Oh, I just don't know what to do.

It's like she pushes me away with one hand and pulls me back with the other. I'm really torn up inside. Tell me, aren't there any other people in this world who have mothers like mine, or is she the only one? Or is it me? Am I the one to blame? Is it my fault? I just can't figure it out.

T. You say that no matter what you did in a situation like this, you'd wind up hurting her, and that you can't hurt her because she's your mother, right?

C. Yeah, that's right. I mean, how can you hurt your own mother?

T. The fact that she's your mother seems to give her an awful lot of power over you, don't you think? I wonder why it is that just the fact of being your mother gives her so much power.

The therapist has posed a question that may be a great aid to the client in his attempt to change his life situation. By exploring and examining his values and the place his mother holds in those values, he may be able to understand the control his mother has over him. Further, he may be able to come to some understanding of why his mother behaves the way she does. The experience will undoubtedly be long and tortuous, but it may lead to the client's ability to see the alternatives open to him, evaluate the consequences of these alternatives, and then to act, and thereby change.

By this point, the reader has probably concluded that parents are "the root of all evil." This is not necessarily true. While the importance and significance of the effects of parents on the personality development of children cannot be denied, too often we find that children "use" their parents as excuses or "cop-outs," so that the troubled individual can say, "It's all my parents' fault. They made me the way I am." The psychotherapy client who takes this position is saying, in essence, "I am the way I am because my parents made me this way. It's their fault and their problem, not mine. Therefore, it is not my responsibility. Since I am not responsible for the way I am, I am also not responsible for changing."

In this way, parents become scapegoats for the individual who wants to escape the pain involved in analyzing his behavior and trying to change himself. These are the clients who often expect the therapist to change the world for them, since they do not want the responsibility or the burden of changing themselves to get along better in the world. For such individuals, psychotherapy is useless; they represent the very opposite—the negation—of the therapeutic process. The client's acceptance of responsibility for his own behavior and his willingness to be responsible for attempting to change are implicit to successful psychotherapy. If the client cannot meet these demands, therapy is fruitless and he need not bother consulting a therapist, for he can be of no help.

Such a situation is illustrated in the following excerpt from a therapy interview with a nineteen-year-old male.

Therapist. I find myself wondering what your goals are, as far as therapy is concerned. It's unclear to me as to what you want to accomplish here.

Client. Well, I can understand that, because I'm not all that sure myself. I guess I want to feel better about my life. I guess that's about as close as I can come to describing my goals in therapy—just to feel better about my life.

T. How do you think that goal can be achieved?

C. Well, I really don't know. Isn't that what I'm here for? Isn't that what you're supposed to tell me?

T. What do you see as being wrong with your life now?

C. Basically, I think that it all stems from the way my parents raised me.

T. Your parents?

C. Yes. I've given all this a lot of thought, you know, and I really feel that they messed me up pretty good.

T. Messed you up?

C. Yes. They raised me to be the way I am. They taught me that life was easy, and that all I had to do was be myself, and that everything good in life would come to me. Basically, that's it. They taught me that I was the greatest thing in the world. That the world owed me something. I found out that they were wrong, and I guess that the reason I'm here is to get fixed up. To find out why I can't seem to make it. It's really been pretty bad. I don't have any friends and I don't have any skills, like abilities, so I can't hold down a job very easily. I've had lots of jobs, but they never seem to work out. Boy, did my parents screw me up. "Be yourself," they said. "Everyone has got to like you if you only be yourself." Well, I am myself, and I like it the way I am, only I just can't seem to succeed at anything. I wish they would've told me something besides just to be myself.

T. You say that you have no friends.

C. Yeah, that's right. Oh, sure, I used to have some buddies, but they couldn't accept me for what I am, and if that's the way they want to be, the hell with them. I don't need friends like that.

T. It sounds like you're pretty mad at everybody—your parents, your friends.

C. Well, I'm sure as hell not happy with them. They weren't real friends anyway—not when they can't accept me for what I am. And my parents, all this is their fault. You don't expect me to be happy about them, do you?

T. I guess what I'm getting at is that you don't see any problems in yourself; you see them in others.

C. Well, that may be true, but I really don't think that I'm the one who's at fault. My parents brought me up. They made me the way I am. I can't be responsible for my own childhood, can I?

T. But you're certainly responsible for yourself now.

C. I'm not sure what you mean.

T. What I mean is that you seem to be blaming your parents for making you the way you are, and you don't seem willing to take the responsibility yourself for the way you live now in the present.

C. Well, isn't it true that you're a product of your parents? I mean, that's what everyone says. If that's so, then how can I be the one to take the blame for the way my life is turning out?

T. I gather then, that you don't see any way that you can work toward changing yourself to make things better.

C. Changing myself? I don't know if I can change. I thought that changing me was your job. I mean, if there's something in me that can be changed, isn't that what you're supposed to do?

T. No, I can't change you. All I can do is show you how to find out what needs to be changed, and how you might go about it. But I can't change you. You have to do that for yourself. Now the first thing that has to be made clear is that you have to be able to see that you have some responsibility for running your own life. You seem to want to blame everyone else, but that's just a big cop-out, because you have to come to recognize your part in all this if you want to change yourself. If you can't do that, then maybe we're just wasting your time as well as mine.

C. But I wouldn't be this way if it weren't for my parents. They . . .

T. (breaking in). There you go again, copping out. Look. You can't use your parents as excuses for what you do. They don't control you. You control yourself, and the sooner you recognize that, the better off you'll be. Now, if I can help, I'd be more than happy to try. But you have to do most of the work.

For clients such as this, therapy becomes little more than one excuse after another, and little progress can be made until the excuses end and the client comes to grips with his own difficulties. It is, in a way, a sad commentary on society that parents serve as one of the most popular excuses for their children's problems.

CHAPTER 6

"Jack and Jill Went Up
the Hill . . ."

At some time or other, strain develops in every marriage. Culturally, this fact is joked about and everyone gets a chuckle from a husband's apparent exasperation with his wife's fickleness. In most marriages, arguments come and go; the couple fights a bit, resolves the conflict and once again "marital bliss" prevails. This is not the pattern in all marriages, however, as the current divorce rates indicate. Nevertheless, in many cases divorce is not the route of solution that a couple takes. Many persons with marital difficulties enlist the aid of a counselor or psychotherapist. Since therapy with married couples is becoming more common, it is treated as a separate category of family therapy (see Chapter 4).

In essence, a man and a woman create a new entity when they marry. The marriage takes on a personality and a character all its own—it is something more than the sum of its parts. Both partners gain a great deal from the relationship —things such as love, physical comfort, sexual contact, and security. Both, however, must give up a great deal and change in many ways if the new entity, the marriage, is to survive. If *he* were not used to rolling the tube of toothpaste and *she,* to squeezing it, there would be no conflict in the bathroom each morning. Each marriage begins with many such minor differences in attitudes and habits and, in its evolution, the marriage is able to absorb the stresses and strains.

Emotional differences and differences in needs, however, are often not as easily discernible and not so whimsical as a toothpaste tube schism. Each partner's personality is complex, and the manner in which the personalities in a marriage interact is of astronomical complexity. Stemming from this unfathomable interaction are familiar statements such as "my wife just doesn't understand me" or "what more does he want from me?"

Questions of this kind reflect what may be the generally accepted idea that when there is marital discord, someone is to blame. Certainly, each partner in a marriage contributes to the conflicts, but as the old song goes, "It takes two to tango." The problem, as a therapist would see it, lies not in the man's behavior or in the woman's, but in their relationship. Because the therapist sees the relationship itself as the "problem," it is often useless to treat marital difficulties by seeing only one partner.

Therapists deal with this problem in different ways. Most frequently, however, the procedure involves interviews with the husband and wife separately, followed by meetings with both partners. The order in which this procedure is followed strongly depends upon the partner who makes the initial contact. In the transcription that follows, the wife, Mrs. J., a twenty-three-year-old woman, has arranged to see a psychotherapist about problems she has been having with her husband. The initial excerpt is taken from the first meeting with the client.

Client.　I can't make him happy with anything I do. . . . He's losing interest in me emotionally and sexually and I can't do anything to stop him. . . . We try to talk but we can't.

Therapist.　Mrs. J. You've spoken about how you think your husband feels, but you can't really see into his mind. Why don't we spend a little more time talking about how you feel about the marriage right now.

C.　I'm doing all I can to make him happy, doctor. I try to make his favorite foods. I get dressed up when he comes home from work at night. Nothing seems to please him any more.

T. You're still talking about him, Mrs. J.

C. I guess you're trying to see whether I'm to blame for any of the trouble. I guess I am . . . I don't know . . . we just can't talk anymore.

T. Mrs. J., how do you feel about your husband?

C. What? . . . I . . . I love him, of course. That's sort of a strange question to ask me.

T. Why?

C. Well, I don't know it's just sort of hard for me to talk about my feelings about him.

T. Yes, it is kind of hard to talk about feelings with me. I wonder if you have that same problem with your husband. Tell me, do you ever get really angry at him?

C. Sometimes, but not too often. He's hard to get mad at.

T. What do you do when you become angry?

C. Oh, I usually become sort of quiet . . . I don't say much to him.

T. Do you tell him why you're angry?

C. Come to think of it, I usually don't. He's really a sensitive person and if I tell him I'm mad at him, he might become pretty hurt.

T. Do you think he knows that you're mad, even though you try to hide your feelings?

C. I'm not sure. . . . Sometimes I think he knows because he asks me what's wrong.

T. What do you say then?

C. I usually make up some excuse. I tell him that nothing is wrong or assure him that he's not to blame for the way I feel, or say something else to get him to leave me alone.

In the above excerpt, the therapist discovered that Mrs. J. was really not directing her discussion towards her own feelings but was describing her marital difficulty in terms of her husband's feelings and actions. He felt that there was some reason for Mrs. J.'s being hesitant to express her own feelings. His rather unexpected question concerning Mrs. J.'s feelings toward her husband caught her off guard, and the therapist saw that Mrs. J. was uncomfortable expressing her feelings verbally. The therapist then followed this line of questioning and determined that the client was not only unable to express love easily, but also had difficulty in communicating anger to her husband.

The therapist now knew something of the manner in which Mrs. J. perceived and reacted to her husband and the way that she behaved towards him, but he had little information about the real "client," the relationship itself. Mr. J., a twenty-four-year-old college graduate presently working in an advertising agency in Manhattan, contributed the following information in his first interview with the therapist.

Therapist.   Thank you for coming in today, Mr. J. I think you realize that even though it was your wife who first contacted me for treatment, you are a very important part of the picture since her problem appears to revolve around your relationship with one another.

Client.   I understand that, doctor. I'll be glad to help in any way I can.

T.   Do you have any idea what's been bothering your wife lately?

C.   You know . . . Jill and I always were able to talk about our problems with one another . . . but . . . I don't know . . . within the last six or seven months she's just stopped talking to me about the way she's feeling . . . she doesn't tell me what she's thinking. I'm getting pretty upset by the whole business too, because she doesn't even allow me the privilege of bitching about my day at the office. You know, advertising isn't exactly the easiest busines to make good in. I'm really under a lot of pressure. I guess I might have overused my complaining rights a while back. Maybe she got fed up with all my troubles . . . who knows?

T.   What sort of troubles are you referring to, Mr. J?

C.   Oh, I was getting really tense with my job . . . there was word out that a few new junior executive positions were opening up. I really wanted to be picked for one of them, but no matter what ideas I came up with . . . well, they just didn't strike the bosses like I'd hoped they would.

T.   And how did this affect your relationship with your wife?

C. Well, for a while, she was really great . . . I could come home and complain to her and tell her how upset I was about the job and she was always sympathetic to me . . . then . . . then she kind of stopped listening. Maybe, well, maybe, I didn't really give her a chance to get things off her chest, maybe that made her mad . . . I don't know.

T. You say that might have made her mad . . . how do you know when she is mad?

C. Well, she just kinda sits down really quietly and reads a book or something . . . she doesn't want to talk to me and doesn't want me to talk to her.

T. How do you find out what she is mad about?

C. Well . . . hey, that really gets me . . . it's strange you brought it up. I go over to her and I say, "What's wrong, Jill" and she says "Nothing" . . . you know what, doctor? When she says "Nothing" I know something's wrong. Then starts the little question and answer period. "Is it something I did?" "It's really nothing." "Why are you so quiet?" "I just feel like it." If I'm lucky, I get to find out some reason for her being mad. If I'm not lucky, things just stay as they were before; I wonder why she's mad and she won't tell me.

T. That seems like a very frustrating experience. But you have left out what you do as a result of your little tête-à-têtes. How do you act after you have been unable to find out the reason for Jill's being mad?

C. At first I feel that I should try to find out what's wrong with her. If it's something I did, I want to know so I can change the way I act. But . . . I don't know if I'm right in feeling this way . . . after ten or fifteen minutes of this questioning I just say the hell with it. I just get really mad at her.

T. What do you do when you get mad at her?

C. Nothing . . . I just kind of grit my teeth and it goes away.

T. What do you think you would like to do with your anger—maybe you'd like to beat the daylights out of your wife for frustrating your attempts to help her.

C. . . . I really never would do something like that, but sometimes I really think about it.

T. What is there about your wife that makes it hard for
you to express anger against her?

C. I don't know, I just can't yell at her . . . she cries . . .
that's worse than her sitting and moping.

T. Mr. J., the situation you describe to me seems to be
one in which your wife is acting like a great martyr
and you are avoiding expressing anger toward her because you think she is suffering enough.

C. You mean I'm afraid to hurt her any more by telling
her that I'm angry with her, so I just forget about it.

T. That's the way it seems . . . but does it really ever go
away? . . . The anger I mean.

At this point, the discussion between Mr. J. and the
therapist will probably begin to focus more on Mr. J.'s feelings, his anger, his modes of expression. But the therapist
has gained a great deal of information.

Initially, the therapist got the feeling that Mr. J. was
anxious to help in his wife's treatment and understood that
he played a great part in his wife's difficulties. It soon became clear to the therapist, however, that some of the difficulties in the marriage were caused by Mr. J.'s behavior
when pressured at work. The therapist seemed to be finding
that Mr. J. overcomplained early in the marriage (he was
under much stress and worry at work) and as a result, Mrs.
J. had not been allowed the prerogative of having problems
of her own.

Apparently, Mrs. J. assumed a role of martyrdom and
became angry or upset. Consequently, she refused to discuss
the problem with her husband—a very frustrating situation
for the couple. Such behavior drives a couple farther and
farther from one another.

But the therapist has not yet seen the couple as a unit.
Therefore, he arranges a meeting with both Mr. and Mrs. J.

Therapist. Well, I've had a chance to talk to both of you
on separate occasions and I've gotten your ideas about
the problem that you're facing in your marriage. Today, let's try to explore the problem a little farther.

Mr. J. Things haven't changed much since I saw you, doctor. Jill still seems very upset, and I just can't figure out why.

T. Is that the way it is, Mrs. J.?

Mrs. J. I guess that's the way Jack sees it.

T. You're still having some trouble talking about how *you* feel, Mrs. J. You talk of your husband's perceptions but make no mention of your own.

Mrs. J. Well, I'm the problem in the family, aren't I? If Jack isn't happy, then I'm still doing something wrong. I'm trying . . . but nothing helps.

T. Mrs. J. it seems that you're feeling too sorry for yourself to even try to pay attention to how you feel towards your husband and your marriage.

Mrs. J. Well, Jack's told you things are still bad, and they are.

T. You think they are?

Mrs. J. Yes . . . oh, what's wrong with us, Jack?

Mr. J. I don't know, Hon, maybe the doctor can tell us.

T. I think you just now came together on something. You've both decided to admit you can't help yourselves and you want me to fix your marriage. It's not that easy.

Mr. J. Well, what should we do here . . . what should we talk about?

T. Why don't you try talking to your wife about your problems?

Mr. J. Well . . . O.K., if you think that's the way to do it . . . (A few minutes of silence ensues; the couple look at one another, but neither speaks. There appears to be a great deal of tension in the room.)

T. For a couple who've been married as long as you two, you have marked difficulty in talking to one another.

Mr. J. I know what I want to say to Jill, doctor, but I'm afraid to say it.

Mrs. J. (starting to weep). Afraid to say it? Is it that terrible? Oh, my God, what's happened to us?

T. Mr. J. says that he is afraid to say something and immediately, Mrs. J., you assume it's the worst—he hates you, he wants a divorce, he's sorry he married you.

Mrs. J. Well, that's the only thing he'd be afraid to tell me!

T. Let's try to find out what we're speculating on. Mr. J., can you tell your wife what you are afraid to say?

Mr. J.   I wanted to tell her . . . you know what we talked about . . . to tell her that I get so damn mad when she doesn't tell me what's bothering her and I have to ask question after question . . . and that I feel like . . . like beating the hell out of her.

T.   You didn't look at your wife when you said that, but the message was obviously for her ears, and not mine.

Mr. J.   I just couldn't say it to her face.

Mrs. J.   Why, Jack?

Mr. J.   (turning to his wife). Because I was afraid that you would be hurt or mad or . . . I don't know.

Mrs. J.   Am I that terrible that you feel like hitting me?

T.   Mrs. J., I don't think that that is what your husband said to you.

Mr. J.   Yeah, Jill . . . listen . . . what I meant was that I really want to find out what's bothering you, and when I can't, I really get frustrated and . . . you know, when a guy gets frustrated he just wants to hit something . . . to break something.

Mrs. J.   You mean to tell me that you really care about how I feel . . . that you really give a damn about my being upset or worried. I know that things at work are really hard on you, Jack (sobbing) . . . but, there's a limit to how much I can listen to your problems before I need someone to listen to mine. I was always there to listen to yours, but you were too upset to hear mine. I just stopped telling you what was wrong with me . . . and I don't care about your old job . . . if you got fired tomorrow, I'd be happy.

Mr. J.   But, I try to do well for you . . . to give you all the things you want.

Mrs. J.   Oh, Jack, don't you see . . . it probably sounds corny, but I really just want us to be happy, the way we used to be. The way things are now, I'm always mad at you and now I find out you're always mad at me. Some happily married couple, we are.

T.   In the last few moments, you've told each other more than you have in months, I'll wager. And isn't it amazing to see that thunder hasn't struck and that both of you are still composed rather than hysterically crying and weeping after having destroyed your mate with your words.

Mrs. J. But, doctor, we've told one another that we're always angry . . . what good is that? We can't live together like that.

T. Of course not.

Mr. J. I don't know about you, Jill, but for some reason, I feel really good right now . . . almost as if I don't care if you're mad at me . . . it's like I'm just glad you told me finally.

Mrs. J. I wish I could say that, Jack, but . . . I feel hurt . . . really, hurt.

Mr. J. About what?

Mrs. J. I don't know . . . I . . . I think I've really failed you as a wife. I knew you needed someone to listen to you . . . but . . . I was so selfish about my wants that I got mad at you for not satisfying me.

T. I think that you've both reached an important point in our discussion. Both of you are finally telling each other how *you* are feeling rather than guessing how the other feels. It seems to me that you can tell each other things a lot easier that way.

Mrs. J. I think I know what Jack meant a few moments ago, doctor. It really seems a lot easier to talk that way.

Mr. and Mrs. J. seem well on their way to reestablishing their relationship. They have been able to tell each other what has been bothering them for so long. Once they said that they were angry, much of the fear of talking to each other disappeared. The therapist was quick to commend them for doing this, encouraging them to be honest with each other more often.

The relationship between the couple in the above example was the target of the therapist's efforts. Initially, it appeared that Mr. and Mrs. J. were unable to use their relationship to solve their problems. That is, their established relationship made no allowance for the expression of negative emotions about one another: this type of talk was just not part of their "ground-rules." Of course, negative emotions develop in any kind of relationship sooner or later, and if there is no appropriate route for their expression, they become pent up. The more pent up they become, the more difficult it is to pass them off. This appeared to be happening in the J.'s marriage. Initially, Mrs. J. was angry because her husband always complained and never listened. She stopped listening because she was angry, but she continued to feel sorry for her husband because of the problems he continued to encounter at work. In her martyr-like fashion, she decided not to bother him with her anger. Mr. J., feeling some positive emotion toward his wife, tried to determine the reasons for her apparent unhappiness. At this point, she chose not to tell him. This resulted in his being frustrated and angry. At this point, both members in the marital relationship were angry and neither could, or would, tell the other. Thus, the marriage had reached an impasse.

Luckily, Mr. and Mrs. J. did not choose to perceive the impasse as a sign that they should seek a divorce. Even though they actually solved the problem themselves in the long run, the therapist they consulted guided them toward a relationship that was free of the limitations on emotional expression that had crippled it.

CHAPTER 7

"I Guess I'm Pretty Mixed Up About Sex"

Since the sexual relationship is a major area in which difficulties can occur, it is with some degree of validity that people often associate the process of psychotherapy with discussions of sexual problems. This is not to say that everyone who enters psychotherapy has sexual problems—this book includes chapters dealing with many other problem areas. However, society's attitude toward sex has made it likely that many individuals will encounter some difficulties in this area at some time in their lives.

For several reasons, the entire concept of the sexual relationship has been encompassed by the umbrella that we refer to as "morality." Society values the control, restriction, and suppression of sexual behavior: an individual who behaves in accordance with such values is "good;" the individual who expresses his sexuality without control, restriction, or regard to such values is "bad." Thus, sexuality, and its expression, are equated with "evil." It is interesting to note that in the time of Chaucer, "swear" words were those that took the name of God in vain, while no value judgments were placed on words that described the parts of the human body or their functions. In more "modern" times, however, few bat an eye when the name of God is used in vain, but specific parts of the body or their functions are regarded as unmentionable "swear" words. Such words are carefully kept from the ears of children lest they become corrupted, and the stories that concern sex are whispered secretively and referred to as dirty jokes or off-color stories. Truly, sex is viewed as inherently evil.

However, man is a sexual being. People are born either male or female, and their sexuality is an inherent part of their existence. Inevitably, the view that sexuality is evil leads to the conclusion that there is a part of man that is evil. He becomes obligated to control and quell this evil part of his makeup. When he has children, he must instill in them an awareness that sexuality is evil and must be controlled. As a result, sex is viewed with conflicting emotions. On one hand, we all have sexual feelings and appropriate sets of sexual behaviors that must be expressed in some way; on the other hand, we are led to believe that these feelings and behaviors are evil. It is not surprising that whenever we experience these normal sexual feelings, we feel that we are evil and have transgressed a moral code.

Sexual problems develop under the stress of guilt and shame we feel for allowing our sexuality to be aroused. Such problems often have their start in childhood when the child becomes aware of his own body and the bodies of others. Parents often react to the child's attempt to explore his body by telling him that he is "bad," that he is doing "wrong," or that he must stop his explorations because it is "dirty." The situation gets worse when the child begins to masturbate. Some parents tell their children that sexual activity causes blindness, insanity, or other disabilities. The child comes to fear his natural impulses and the psychological consequences of such fear are far more real and devastating than the fairy tales that he has been told by his parents. It is not unusual, in fact, for a young male to ask for psychotherapy in the belief that he is perverted because he masturbates twice each week. Such behavior is well within normal limits, and the wise therapist can deal with the client's fears simply by referring him to a good book on the subject.

Another problem that is often as easy to deal with concerns the individual who seeks psychotherapy because he is afraid he is a homosexual. He remembers engaging in sexual play with another male of the same age when he was five or six years old and concludes that he must be abnormal. Such experiences are very common; in fact, they teach a child to understand the parts of his body that his parents are so reluctant to talk about. Heterosexual "games" that young children play also serve this purpose, and by no means indicate a tendency toward perversion.

However, there are too many sexual problems that cannot be dealt with by simply supplying facts. The number and degree of severity of such difficulties are great, and the amounts of guilt and shame associated with them are greater still. The extraordinarily high degree of conflict associated with sexuality makes it extremely difficult for an individual with sexual problems to seek help. Fears of being a sex maniac or a pervert make the discussion of sexual matters difficult for men as well as for women, but especially for men. Men experience extreme difficulties regarding sex because of the popular conception of what a man is like.

Little boys learn very quickly that a man is expected to be strong, charming, aggressive, and virile. Males in our society are subjected to a great deal of pressure to conform to this image. Certainly, "sissy" is one of the most feared invectives that can be hurled at a little boy by his peers, and, as most high school students will confirm, the boys who are the most socially active are usually those who are the most athletic, "masculine" specimens.

Inherent in the notion of masculinity is the attribute of "virility." The male who is viewed as masculine is often thought of as being sexually capable. Thus, for any male, sexual performance is an indication of masculinity. Sexual behavior, for men, often represents the essence of their manhood, and the stress on males to perform well sexually is always present. Inadequacy, or the inability to perform well, presents a crisis to one's identity as a male, and the consequences may be devastating in all spheres of life.

The first excerpt in this chapter deals with a young male who finds that he is unable to achieve an erection when he attempts to have sexual intercourse with his wife. This young man found it very difficult to enter treatment because

he feared that the therapist would laugh at him for his inade-
quacies, but he has reached the conclusion that he must see
someone for help.

It is important for the reader to note that therapists
who have been trained according to different theories of human behavior may view problems somewhat differently.
Some may view a problem as the result of deep-seated difficulties—that problems are merely symptoms of more underlying causes. Other therapists, however, may view a problem
not as a symptom of an underlying "disease," but as the entire problem in and of itself. In either case, the initial task
of the client is the same. He must be as explicit as possible
about the problem, including such issues as when it began,
when it occurs, and how long it lasts. Hopefully, these issues
will be made clear by the interviews presented.

Client.   I know that I have to tell you all about it, but it's
        very hard. Some things are almost too embarrassing to
        talk about, even in a situation like this.
Therapist.   I can see that it must be really tough for you,
        but if we can't discuss whatever it is that's bothering
        you so much, it's going to be impossible to do anything
        about it.
C.   I know . . . well . . . it's . . . I . . . I think there's
        something wrong with me . . . I mean sexually. It's
        . . . well . . . I can't seem to be able to have sex with
        my wife anymore. I don't understand it, but it's just eat-
        ing away at me, and I'm afraid that it might mess up my
        marriage.
T.   Tell me more about it.
C.   Well, it's been going on for about two months now. I
        just get upset or something every time we try to have
        sex, and nothing happens.
T.   Nothing happens?
C.   Well, it . . . like . . . it doesn't work out right. I mean,
        I just get this awful feeling in the pit of my stomach,
        and then I can't get excited. I don't know why. Some-
        times, when I do get excited, I don't stay that way. As
        soon as we start to make love, I get that feeling again
        in my stomach. My wife has really been understanding

and all, but I'm afraid that she won't be able to take too much more of this.

T. Tell me about the feeling you get in your stomach. Is it like any other feelings you've had before?

C. Well, it's an upset kind of feeling, like I used to get sometimes when I was in school and I had to stand up in front of my class and give a speech . . . like stage fright, I guess. I used to feel that way when I had to take exams too. It's just an uncomfortable feeling, deep inside my stomach.

T. The examples you give me sound like what you're feeling is some kind of a fear.

C. Fear? Well, maybe, but why should I be afraid? We've been married for over three years now, and I've never had any trouble like this before.

T. You say that this started about two months ago. What was going on at that time?

C. Uh . . . nothing that I can really think of. Nothing special or out of the ordinary . . . well, let me think for a minute. (Silence, 30 seconds.) Well, I'm not sure whether this is the kind of thing you're looking for, but it was about that time when we started talking about having a family. We've been living it up since we got married, and my wife thinks that it's time to settle down and start a family.

T. It sounds like you don't agree with her.

C. No. I do agree. After all, it would be nice to be fairly young when we have children, so that we could be close to them as they grow up.

T. Is that you talking, or is that what your wife says.

C. (laughing). I guess it's what she said. But I think she's right. It's nice to be close to your kids in age. You can share a lot more with them that way.

T. Had you been thinking about starting a family before she brought it up?

C. Not exactly. I mean, I knew that some day we'd have children, but I really hadn't given it much thought before she mentioned it. I'm afraid I don't understand what you're getting at.

T. Well, let's pull everything you've told me together for a minute. You've been married for several years, and things seem to have been going quite well for you. About two months ago, your wife mentions the fact that she'd like to start raising a family, and at that time, you begin experiencing difficulties in your sexual relationship with her. Do you think there's any connection?

C. I see. You're saying that I'm having this problem because my wife wants children and I don't, is that it?

T. Actually, I'm asking you, not telling you. I just wonder whether that strikes you as a possibility.

C. But I do want to have children . . . at least I think I do.

T. I don't want to put ideas into your head that aren't true. Maybe you could tell me something about how the issue was raised at the time, and how you reacted.

C. Well, let's see. I came home from work . . . it was a murderous day. Everything seemed to be going wrong at work. Anyway, I came home, and we had dinner, and then we sat down to watch TV, and we were watching this show about kids. I can't remember the name of the show. Anyway, we were watching this show, and she said something like, "don't you think it's time that we started having children?" I guess I was pretty surprised. It took me a few seconds to realize what she said. It was pretty unexpected. I guess I told her that it was O.K. with me, since we had enough money and all. She was all smiles . . . I guess it made her very happy. We didn't talk any more about it, but the next time . . . yes . . . the next time we had sex, which was a few days later, I began to have this problem. You know, you may be right. Maybe it is because I don't want children yet. But it's awfully hard for me to really believe that. Oh, I'm just not sure about it now. I mean, I believe that it's possible, but I . . . (silence).

T. Maybe the reason that this explanation of your problem is so hard for you to believe is that you have some other explanation already.

C. Well, no, not really. I just thought . . . well . . . I really don't know. I have no other explanation for it.

T. You just thought what?

C. Nothing, really.

T. I know it's hard, but it might be important to bring out what's on your mind. You did look as if you wanted to say something. Can you try to tell me what it was?

C.   I don't know. I just get these ideas about myself sometimes. I mean, I always thought that guys who have problems like this were . . . well . . . sick. I mean . . . you know . . . perverted or something.

T.   So you think you're perverted?

C.   Well, isn't it true? I mean, don't problems like this . . . like, when you can't get excited with a woman, doesn't that mean that you're . . . well . . . a homosexual?

T.   Not at all, but I think that you might be hurting yourself a good deal by thinking that you are a homosexual.

C.   I always thought . . . well . . . I was always so proud of myself. My wife and I were always happy with our sex life, but since this started, my life has been a nightmare. It's gotten so that I do all kinds of things to avoid having sex. I pick fights, and pretend I'm mad at her, or I tell her that I'm really tired—too tired, if you know what I mean. Sometimes I'll sit up and watch TV for hours—till four or five in the morning, because I'm afraid that she's waiting up for me. I don't know how much longer things can go on this way. I guess that that's why I came here. My whole life has been affected by this thing. I'm having trouble concentrating at work, and my boss is beginning to get mad. Whenever I go out with my wife, we don't have as much fun as we used to.

As illustrated by the above interview, sexual adequacy often plays a central part in the life of a male. The individual who does not measure up to the societal view of masculinity may automatically view himself as a total failure. This self-doubt is reflected in almost every aspect of his life. It is not uncommon for men who experience sexual difficulties to label themselves homosexuals or perverts. There simply is no room in the societal view of masculinity for inadequacy. One is either perfect or one is worthless.

Another aspect of sexual inadequacy that often presents major difficulties for males lies in doubts of their masculinity as a result of various phenomena that have been grouped together under the term "sexual incompatibility." This term is quite broad and can include many different problems. One such problem involves the situation in which the male is unable to bring his sexual partner to fulfillment in the sexual experience.

In the past, the societal view of a sexual relationship was such that the woman's sexual fulfillment was secondary to the male's. However, as women began to establish a more aggressive role in society, men became more concerned about ensuring a more satisfying sexual experience for their partners. Unfortunately, education regarding the difference between male and female sexual functioning has been so inadequate that many men do not understand that certain patterns of sexual behavior are inadequate to provide fulfillment for a woman. (For example, males who do not understand that women take longer than men to reach the peak of sexual experience may wonder why they are not desirable sex partners.) This lack of information has been the basis of many fears on the part of males regarding their sexuality, and, therefore, their masculinity.

Again, it must be stressed that problems involving actual or suspected sexual inadequacy are devastating to males because their sexuality is so deeply a part of their role in society. Before he will consult a psychiatrist, the man with a sexual problem must find the anxiety and pain he suffers more unbearable than the torture of admitting he needs help. The simple admission that help is necessary is, for most males, a reflection of their inadequacy. The next interview illustrates a situation in which such a problem has culminated in a situation that may lead to the breakup of a marriage. A husband and wife have come to see a therapist as a "last resort" before proceeding with their plans for a divorce. They have two children and claim that they want to try to make the marriage work "for the children's sake." The problems they see in their marriage are great and, although their sexual relationship is considered "one of our problems," it is not seen as the major problem. Again, it is important to note that sexual problems may affect all aspects of an individual's life—not just sex—and the couple whose interview is presented here is beginning to realize how the sexual difficulty has, in fact, had a major destructive effect on their relationship.

Therapist.   So it seems like sex isn't as minor a factor in all this as you've thought.

Wife.   Mmh, yes, I would say that it's been important, but I don't see how sex alone could account for all the troubles we've been having. I mean, it's gotten so that I dread the minute he comes home from work because I know that we'll just get into another fight. I mean, we haven't had sex in so long that I've forgotten what it's like, not that I'd care to remember particularly. So, if we never even consider sex, how can it be responsible for all the problems we've been having?

T.   You say that you don't particularly care to think about your past sexual experiences. Were they that bad?

Husband   (cutting in). Aw, come on, let's not go through all that again. Look, we're not getting anywhere this way. My wife's right. We haven't even thought of sex in so long that it couldn't have anything to do with all the crap we've been talking about.

T.   Why is it so important for you to believe that?

H.   Huh? What do you mean?

T.   Well, you've both been trying awfully hard to convince me that sex is really not the major problem for you. I wonder if you find it that important to convince yourselves of that.

W.   But all the misery that we've been going through has been going on for so long, and we haven't even thought about sex for so long—I mean, it hasn't even been in the picture, so how could it be so important?

T.   Maybe the answer to that lies in the kinds of experiences you've had with sex in the past. You've said that you weren't particularly happy about them. Could you tell me more about that?

H.   It was always pretty bad. Well, not always. I mean, when we first got married, things were pretty good, I thought. I mean, we were pretty happy then.

T.   You mean your sex life was pretty good.

H.   Yeah, and we enjoyed it, too. I'd come home from work, and she'd have a drink ready for us, and then we'd go to bed. It was great—just the way I'd always pictured married life. I just don't know what happened.

W. He's right there, at least about the beginning. We were pretty happy. But after about a year, things began to change.

T. Change?

W. Yes. I really can't explain it. I guess that I just got tired of it—sex, I mean. I . . . I don't know. It just wasn't what I thought it would be. I mean (laughs) you see all these movies and read all these books, and I thought it would be like that.

T. What was it like in the movies that was different than the way you experienced it?

W. Well, I don't know exactly. I mean, well, in the movies, you always got the feeling that they were—well—I don't know the right word—like it was the greatest moment in their lives, like, oh, I can't explain it.

H. You see, doc, she was always talking about the movies, and why couldn't it be that way with us. As if anybody else would've been better (laughs). She couldn't understand that the movies all played it up, like it could really be like that, right?

T. You don't think it could've been better?

H. Aw, come on. She wants a superman. She thinks that the guys in the movies are for real.

T. It sounds a little like you're afraid that they might just be for real.

H. Look, when I was a bachelor, I used to make all the girls happy. I was great. There must be something wrong with my wife, because no one else I was ever with ever said anything about the movies like her. I mean, I'm not superman or anything, but I can sure go with the best of 'em.

T. So you think that the problem must have been with your wife.

H. I don't really know—I guess it must be—she must be, like, oversexed or something.

T. Oversexed?

H. Yeah, oversexed. I guess that's what you call it . . . isn't that what you call it when a woman sort of . . . well . . . can't get . . .

W. Satisfied, you mean?

H. What's that supposed to mean?

W. That's the word you were looking for, isn't it?

H. See, doc? This is what I mean when I tell you that we get into fights. She always does this kind of thing.

T. What kind of thing?

H. Well, you heard her. I was trying to be serious—to try and express my feelings, like you said I should—and she makes fun of me.

T. Sounds like she might've hit on something that you find pretty upsetting.

H. Now you're taking her side.

T. All I said was that something that she said is upsetting to you. Is that taking anyone's side?

H. No, I guess not. Oh, how did we get into this mess, any-how?

T. You were saying that you felt that your wife was over-sexed, and she seemed to suggest that she just wasn't satisfied when you had sex. Is that right?

H. Yeah, I guess that's possible, but I don't understand why I never had that kind of trouble with any other girl.

W. You were never married to any other girl.

H. What does that have to do with it?

W. Maybe with all the others, just the once-in-a-while ex-citement of having sex was enough, but when we got married, it wasn't once in a while anymore, and the fun of just having sex wasn't enough. I wanted something more, but you never seemed to pay attention to that.

H. That's not true. You were just too oversexed, that's all.

In the above excerpt, the husband's behavior clearly il-lustrates the man's difficulty in openly dealing with his feel-ings of sexual inadequacy. Yet, the only way to resolve such difficulties is to talk about them. In time, as the husband becomes better able to talk about his discomfort over the possibility that he may not, in fact, be able to satisfy his wife, the therapist can help by providing some information about sexuality, thus enabling both husband and wife to realize that there is nothing wrong with either of them as far as sexuality is concerned. Again, the crucial factor is the hus-band's ability to overcome the shame he obviously feels and to trust that neither the therapist nor his wife will deride him for his problem.

While the incidence of sexual problems is higher in

males than females, a phenomenon attributable, in part, to our culture, females are by no means free of sexual problems. Many of the problems that females encounter are products of societal indoctrination, much as with males. Females are taught from early childhood that it is the responsibility of the woman to say "no" in sexual matters. They are taught that the male is the aggressive partner, while the female must try her best to control the male's advances. They are taught that sex before marriage is bad and that sex must be reserved for the right man at the right time. The girl who, for one reason or another, breaks one of these taboos, finds herself ridden with guilt and shame—a circumstance that can cause any one of several sexual problems in the future.

One such problem will now be illustrated in an excerpt of an interview with a twenty-one-year-old female who, after two months of marriage, has found that she is unable to engage in sexual relations with her husband. At the age of seventeen she had had intercourse with a man whom she never saw after she spent the night with him, even though they had been dating for several months prior to that experience. She has seen the therapist several times and is talking about her attitudes toward sex.

Client. . . . and you have this, like . . . like a switch inside you that you're supposed to keep on all the time until you get married, no matter what happens. It doesn't matter how long you've been dating a guy, or how you feel about each other. You just have that switch inside you that you're supposed to keep on all the time. Then, when you get married, you just turn the switch off, I guess. But I just can't turn off the switch. I turned it off once, when I was 17, and I haven't been the same since. I don't know what to do.

Therapist.   What happens when you try to have sex now?

C.   Well, I think that my husband's almost given up. We've tried lots of times, but I sort of get this cold, clammy feeling, like I'm doing something terrible, and I can't stand to have him come near me. I guess maybe . . . maybe I . . . don't . . . I guess maybe I don't . . . love him (crying).

T. You think that if you really loved him you wouldn't react this way.

C. Well, what else is there to think? I mean, he is my husband, and if I can't let him near me, I guess there's nothing else to believe, is there?

T. You think that there's some magic that happens with the right guy that will make it so that you won't feel this way.

C. I don't know if it's magic or not, but how can I love him if I feel like this whenever I get near him?

T. Was it always like this with him?

C. No, before we were married, we had this . . . well, we had this understanding. We agreed that we wouldn't have sex until after we were married. There was no problem then . . . I mean, we petted and all, but I never had this feeling like I get now.

T. Does the feeling you're talking about go away when your husband decides to leave you alone?

C. Yes, it goes away when I convince him that I can't go through with it. It takes me about half an hour, but then I'm fine again. My husband thinks that there's something really wrong with me, like he said that I'm frigid. Am I frigid, doctor?

T. You told me before that you once did have sexual intercourse. Could you tell me more about that?

C. Yes. Like I said, it was when I was 17. I had been going out with this boy for a few months, and I really loved him, or at least I thought I did. He said he loved me too, and, well, you know, one thing led to another, and we wound up in bed. I really don't remember too much about it. I was scared as hell, and it was over fast. You know, sometimes I get the feeling like it was just a bad dream, like it never happened at all. But it did. Anyway, we were in a motel, and after we . . . after we had sex, he took me home and never called me again. I felt terrible. I wanted to kill myself. My mother, it was like she could read my mind. She seemed to know exactly what happened. She called me every name in the book, and then some. It's a good thing she didn't tell my dad, because it would've just killed him. I was always his little darling—his baby girl. He would've just died. Anyway, my mother cursed me out for about an hour, and then she stomped out of my room, and I cried for the rest of the day. It was like I was afraid to go out, like people could see it written on my face. I was so embarrassed and so ashamed that I couldn't face anybody. I guess that's when I turned my switch back on again, and now I can't turn it off. I told my husband about this whole episode before we got married. He really was great when I told him. He said that it could've happened to anybody, and it would be stupid to hold it against me now. That was before we got married. Since our wedding, he's brought it up lots of times. He's really bothered by it. He says I don't love him. How can I make him understand? Or is he right—maybe I don't love him. I guess I'm pretty mixed up.

Again, it is clear that sexual problems seem to affect functioning in many areas of life. The woman in the above excerpt came to the conclusion that she did not love her husband because of the guilt and shame she felt regarding a sexual encounter years earlier. Such situations are not uncommon, and, as with other kinds of problems, the client's task is to be able to talk as openly as possible about the difficulty.

Another form of sexual problem experienced by women is illustrated by a twenty-six-year-old unmarried secretary, who has been using sex to "try and get a husband." She has confused pure sexuality with affection, and in her attempts to hold men by having sexual relations with them, she has neglected to develop relationships with them on a more meaningful level. The excerpted interview that will now be presented illustrates a most important aspect of psychotherapy. The client is discussing the pattern that her relationships with men have followed. Much of our behavior follows patterns. Most times, we are not aware of these patterns. However, when a particular pattern of behavior frequently results in our being hurt or upset, it helps to become aware of the pattern so that it can be broken. The therapist helps the client to see such patterns, and enables the client to consider alternate ways of behaving, but it is the client who must actually make the change.

Client. Well, with Jim, it was pretty much the same as with the others. We met through a mutual friend, and Jim asked me out to a movie. After the movie, we got something to eat, and then we went back to my place. We talked for a while, and I really started to like him. When we started to (laughs) get a little friendlier, I remember saying to myself that I shouldn't get carried away again, but I always do, no matter how hard I try. Well, the rest is obvious. He never called again. I couldn't for the life of me think why, but I can't say I didn't expect it. It had happened so many times before that I really had no reason to believe that this time would be any different.

Therapist. So, we have the same pattern again. You meet, go out, come back to your apartment, talk for a while, and then have sex.

C. Right. It's always the same.

T. What would happen if you didn't have sex with one of the guys you meet?

C. What would happen? I don't know. I'm not sure what you mean.

T. Well, for example, what would you do instead? Let's say you came back to your apartment with a date, started to talk, and decided that you weren't going to sleep with him. What would you do? What else is there to a relationship between a man and a woman besides sex?

C. Well . . . I guess there's . . . uh . . . companionship?

T. Are you asking me or telling me?

C. Telling you, I guess.

T. What do you mean by companionship?

C. Just being together, talking or something like that, I suppose.

T. Talking?

C. Yes, but I don't see how that's any different from what I've been doing all along. I mean, we always talk for a while.

T. About what?

C. Well, it's usually about the movie that we saw, or what restaurants are good, or the weather, or where we went to school, or the job—stuff like that.

T. In other words, you make small talk.

C. Yes, I suppose it is small talk, but how else do you start things going?

T. I never said that small talk isn't the way to start things going, but I'm wondering what else you see in a relationship with a man besides small talk and sex.

C. (Silence) Well . . . (laughs) I've always wondered, you know . . . well, it's a little embarrassing, but I've always wondered what people who are married talk about, or what they do.

T. You know, I'm getting the impression that sex is something you do when you run out of small talk.

C. I guess that's right (laughs), but . . . I mean really, I don't know what else to do.

T. Have you ever talked with a man about yourself, or about him? I don't mean things like where you work, or where you went to school. I mean about yourselves—your dreams, your hopes, the things you like in life, and the things you fear as well.

C. Well, not really like that . . . no, I haven't. But guys really aren't interested in that.

T. So all you have to offer a guy is some small talk and sex.

C. That's a little strong. No, I have other things to offer. I'm a good cook, and I like to do things outdoors. I like to go for long walks, especially in the rain. I like museums and art exhibits, and stuff like that. But I really don't think that most guys would be all that turned on to a long walk in the rain with me.

T. How do you know? You've never even tried it.

C. Oh, come on. Guys are after one thing. That's the way the world is, and you have to play by those rules if you want to win the game.

T. But you haven't been winning, have you?

C. Not yet, but some day I will.

To many of her friends and acquaintances, the woman in the above excerpt must seem pretty happy, enjoying her life, and fairly well-adjusted. However, her difficulties are quite serious—perhaps even more serious than the other individuals who have been presented in this chapter. By serious, it is meant that it may take her some time to work out her problems. Even though she has no severe "symptoms,"

as did the man who was impotent or the girl who couldn't
engage in sexual activity with her husband, she has a severe
problem in that she must learn how to relate to men. Her
entire training in how to get along with men was inadequate,
for she learned that relationships do not involve revealing
oneself to another. No doubt, she would consider that she
reveals quite a bit of herself through sex, but this is a mis-
understanding of the meaning of "revealing" oneself. For
her, therapy will involve the necessity of revealing herself
to her therapist, and of using that relationship as a way to
learn about other relationships. The process may be long
and difficult, and there is always a possibility that she will
be unable or unwilling to go through with it; nevertheless,
this is her task in psychotherapy.

CHAPTER 8

"I Must Decide What to Do"

From the time of birth to quite late in adolescence, human beings are said to be dependent upon their parents for direction, nurturance and security. However, during the normal course of development, a child comes to want and need increasing independence; he must learn to make decisions for himself, to feel confident in the decisions he makes, and to be secure in the life he leads. Most individuals establish their state of independence from parental authority and guidance during their adolescence. What seems to be a trial by torture for most parents when their children are teenagers actually can be seen as a necessary process that will make it possible for the offspring to survive as adults after the parents have passed from the picture.

Dependence and independence, its counterpart, are very important dimensions of human functioning. For this reason, it is not enough to deal with them as abstract terms. Rather, we must consider them in reference to particular situations. Thus, we might find that a certain individual is capable of making confident decisions when he is dealing with managerial problems arising during his work but is unable to decide what to do about dealing with his family problems. The point is that whether or not a person is dependent is a function of the situations in which he finds himself.

When people are unable to become, or remain, independent of their parents or other guiding authorities at places and times in their lives when such independence is important and their lack of independence creates feelings of anxiety, depression or inadequacy, the time may have come for them to seek professional help from a psychotherapist. A difficulty, of course, with such a person, is that seeking psychotherapy is for him just another example of his inabilities to do things for himself. It is quite important for a therapist to realize this and to be sure that his relationship does not plunge his client further into a dependent stance.

A twenty-year-old Oriental college sophomore, who referred himself for treatment, will illustrate this example. At the time of his initial interview, it was determined that he felt very depressed, was considering dropping out of college or, even worse, committing suicide. Further inquiry revealed that he was the third of four sons and that each of his two older brothers had gone into professional scientific fields. At the time that he started therapy, the client, Robert, was a chemistry major. Following is an excerpt from a session in which the topic of the client's inability to make decisions was discussed.

Therapist.   Robert, we spoke last time about the fact that you have to decide on a permanent major in a few months and that you can't decide what to do.

Client.   Well, as I said, I wish to become a musician and play piano as a career, but I also like chemistry.

T.   Let's talk a little about why you like music.

C.   I've always loved music . . . I've been playing piano since I was ten years old . . . I've given some recitals at the music school here at the university.

T.   It seems like you're good enough of a pianist to warrant considering music as a profession.

C.   My music teacher tells me that I would be wasting my talents if I gave up music for chemistry.

T.   Why do you have to give up one if you choose the other?

C.   Music and chemistry are both very difficult subjects . . . I would have to devote all of my time to the one I choose.

T.   But you're dividing your time between them, now.

C.   I know, and I must decide . . . I must decide.

T.   Let's find out why you're attracted to chemistry.

C.   Again, I like chemistry . . . I enjoy doing experiments and I enjoy the mathematics of it.

T. Have you wanted to be a chemist for as long as you've dreamed of being a professional pianist?

C. No, but it's a good scientific profession to be in.

T. Sounds like you're saying that it's the same kind of thing that your brothers went into.

C. Well, that's important . . . those professions give you a stable income and they are associated with status at least. There are lots of good chemists and they're recognized as being good, but there aren't that many pianists who become famous and are recognized as being important.

T. From the tone of your last comment, I got the feeling that you really didn't believe what you were saying. It almost sounded as if it were a sort of recorded announcement being said by someone else.

C. Well, you may be right there, those are the points of view of my parents pretty much.

T. Are they important in your decision?

C. Of course.

T. How are they important?

C. They want me to go into something that is going to insure that I'm secure for the rest of my life. I've always listened to them. . . . You know, in my culture it is very important to listen to your parents . . . nobody else seems to have that problem, but I can't go against what they say.

T. I can understand that they want the best for you, but don't you think that at the age of twenty you should start trying to decide things for yourself?

C. Of course, but that's easy to say and hard to do.

T. I have the feeling that you really want to go into music as a profession and that you're almost asking me to tell you to do that.

C. If a doctor tells me that I should do that, it would be easier to convince my parents that I am doing the right thing.

T. Then when you once again come into conflict with your parents about a major decision, you'll be looking for another person with authority to guide you. We might be solving your problems now, but we wouldn't be getting you to a point where you wouldn't need a therapist to help you all the time. It's almost as if you have to listen to a parent figure; if your real parents won't tell you what you want to hear you're going to look for a parent that will.

C. But I must decide.

T. Let's talk about the decision and try to deal with it on a rational basis. What are your positive and negative feelings about going into chemistry?

C. Chemistry is a good profession and I am good at it. When I get time to study all I should, I do well on my tests and lab work.

T. Do you like chemistry enough to spend the rest of your life in that field?

C. . . . No . . . I hate it.

T. So you're really in a bind just with chemistry. Your brothers have chosen similar fields and they apparently have pleased your parents . . . and in order for you to please your parents you are being driven into something you don't like.

C. But I am good at chemistry.

T. But you don't like it as much as music.

C. But music is a stupid profession to go into. There is no guarantee that I will succeed. I do not even know if I can do well or if I am good enough.

T. But you said earlier that your teacher said you could be a good professional pianist.

C. I don't know what to do.

T. What this all seems to come down to is the fact that you are too afraid to go against the wishes of your parents to make any decision about your life. But the fact that you have not completely given up the thought of music as a profession indicates that you are countering your parents' wishes to some extent.

C. It's unfair of them to put me in this position.

T. Now you're blaming them for a position you've put yourself in . . . It's not they who cannot decide, it's you.

C. But what should I do?

T. That's the second time today you've asked me to decide for you and I will once again refuse.

C. Then you can't really help me . . . or you won't.

T. You're beginning to get a little angry at me for not helping you to decide. Sounds like you see me like your par-

ents, and you're showing me the anger you have towards
them.

C. No, I am not really angry at you.

T. Of course you are, but you're afraid to tell me because
you're afraid I might reject you or refuse to help you.
That's the same reason you're not saying anything to
your parents about your indecision and your anger
about feeling forced into chemistry.

C. But what will I do without my parents?

T. Do you think that if you tell them you do not want to go
into chemistry they will forget that you're their son?

Now it seems that the therapist has brought the client
to the point where he must face his dependence on his parents and his fears of rejection squarely.

As was seen in the interview, this young man was quite
clear about his vocational preference, but the fear of rejection by his parents made it impossible for him to choose the
field he was drawn to. His dependency was made even clearer
when he asked the therapist what to do. The therapist
quickly picked this up and pointed out that the client was
asking for parental advice from him. Had the therapist made
the mistake of telling the client to go into music because
that's what he liked best, the client's problems would have
been temporarily solved. He would have been able to counter
his own parents' edicts with the statement of a new, more
powerful parent. This, of course, would have kept him happy
only until he met another situation in which his own wishes
were counter to those of his parents. Then, once again, he
would have been hurled into a tense internal conflict and
deep depression. He would have sought direction again and
his dependence would have remained a problem.

Following several months of psychotherapy, this client
was able to make a decision concerning his future. With the
therapist's aid, he came to realize that his decision could be
a *both* rather than an *either/or*. He decided that he could be
a professional scientist and have security and guaranteed
status and, at the same time, be a musician. Since, as a musician only, should he fail, he would have nothing to fall back

on, he decided to become a chemist but to continue his study of music. Now, he has received his degree in chemistry and given numerous piano recitals that were received with critical praise.

Extreme dependency is, of course, one end of a dimension, its opposite being extreme or abnormal independence. Here we find the individual who needs nobody to help him deal with the problems of life. While the source of this state of affairs in a person may vary, there are several situations that are conducive to its development.

Initially, there is the situation in which a child is brought up in a family that provides no chance for dependence. Here we would find homes in which parents are separated and the parent with whom the child lives demands that the child think and care for himself more than usual. Or a child may find himself in a situation where experience has taught him that his parents are unable to direct him or satisfy his needs any better than he, himself, is able.

Regardless of the actual source of extreme independence, however, this kind of behavior often leads to problems that the extremely independent person must cope with during his life. Often, a person is just *acting* as if he were independent when, actually, he is crying for someone to lean on. He may be afraid to ask people for help because he was rejected in the past; he may not know how to be appropriately dependent because he has never been allowed to be dependent.

The following therapy session deals with Bill, an eighteen-year-old young man who wanted no one's help and did everything for himself. He decided he needed therapy because he had been unable to establish any relationships with females and was unable to go out on dates, as his friends did. At the age of four, Bill had been separated from his mother, who was hospitalized in a state institution as the result of a chronic mental disorder. He lived with his father, a rather unstable man who floated from job to job, and his brother, Alex, who was four years older. In early interviews, Bill said he remembered wanting to have his mother back in the home as a child, but that his father always told him that this could never be. Now, at the age of eighteen, he had come to a point where he wanted nothing to do with his father, saw his mother as a hopeless loss, and was unable to deal with Alex on other than a hostile level.

Therapist. Have things been going any better socially this week?

Client. No. The same thing. I just can't go up to a girl and ask her to go out with me. Maybe I really don't want to.

T. You're probably afraid that she'll say no.

C. Maybe I am, but she won't care if my feelings are hurt.

T. You're talking about a girl, but I bet you'd say the same thing about your mother.

C. My parents never cared, I know that . . . I hate my father . . . but what's that got to do with not asking a girl out?

T. As we've said many times before, you don't like to depend on other people to satisfy your needs. Your parents never did, and I think you feel that if you let yourself get involved with other people, they'll reject you also.

C. I just feel so damn lonesome . . . it's like being locked up in a cage and not being able to get out.

T. You're afraid to get out, but at the same time you don't like being in the cage.

C. So what's that supposed to mean?

T. It means that you're uncomfortable about things regardless of how you decide to act. If you remain alone, you hurt; and you're afraid that if you try to not be alone, you're going to get hurt even more.

C. So what?

T. Now I think that we're starting to talk about something that really hits you where you live. You're getting tense and you're showing it by getting a little angry at me.

C. Well, you don't really care what happens to me . . . you just sit there and talk big and you don't give a damn.

T. Listen to what you're saying, Bill. You've probably wanted to say that to your father at one time or another. The fact is that I'm not your father and that I do care about what happens to you.

C. Why should I listen to you?

T. Something in you tells you not to, but something else in you wants to listen to me.

C. Well, I keep coming to see you every week, there must be some reason for that. But nothing seems to be happening. I feel the same now as I did when we started.

T. It takes a long time to trust someone when you've been unable to for so long.

C. Why should I trust you . . . why should I trust anybody?

T. I can see why you don't trust people . . . people have given you a pretty raw deal . . . especially your family. Do you think you have any trust for them?

C. I've got none for my father, but I sort of wish Alex and I could be closer.

T. Why?

C. He's been able to get through my family without being screwed up like I am. He finished college, which I probably won't; he goes out on dates and gets along well with girls; and he's doing pretty well in the army right now.

T. Sounds like he's been able to cope with life fairly well. How does your father feel about him?

C. Oh, Dad is really proud . . . Alex is a good boy.

T. You say that with sarcasm, but I note a feeling of jealousy.

C. No, I don't care . . . I hate my old man . . . I don't care what he thinks of me . . . he's a no-good drunk . . . he never calls me on the phone unless he's loaded and then he tells me "I love you, Bill" . . . that's a load of bull.

T. Has he ever told you that when he's sober?

C. You kidding . . . he hardly ever talks to me when he's not drunk, except to say Bill, do this; Bill, do that.

T. In a way, you wish that you could get him to really love you . . . to get him to be proud of you like he is of Alex.

C. Whatever you say (sarcastically).

T. That's a good way of telling me that you don't want to talk about something that's important to you emotionally. But I still think that you'd like your father to accept you as a son and to do things for you and with you.

C. Anybody would want that kind of thing with his father, but with my old man . . . forget it.

T. OK, so you can never have a relationship with your father, or anybody else in your family. Does that mean that you can't have relationships with people out of your family?

C. I don't really want any.

T. Now you're saying that you didn't come to see me for any reason . . . that you don't want to be able to function socially.

C. I've been thinking that I'm going to quit school and join the Marines and volunteer for Vietnam.

T. That came out of nowhere. Why did you bring it up now?

C. Well, this whole thing is a waste of time. Nothing's gonna happen. I may as well go out and get myself killed.

T. You probably said that to get me to say don't do it. That way you'd know if I cared about you or not. Another thing is that getting yourself into the Marine Corps will be a way to show your father that you're just as tough, if not tougher, than your brother.

Therapy with Bill continued for several more sessions. He dated several girls, but each time his fear of rejection and pseudo-independent attitude prevented the development of meaningful relationships. Finally, he became more despondent and attempted suicide. After taking a bottle of sleeping pills he immediately called the therapist to tell him what he had done. The therapist arranged to have his stomach pumped and told the client he would see him at the next appointed time. After this occurrence, Bill became a different person. He saw that though the therapist really cared about him, he would not become panicky at his client's childish tantrum behavior. From this point on, Bill was able to relate to the therapist in a more dependent manner. He was dependent enough to allow the therapist to guide him into better ways of dealing with and trusting people. Finally, Bill was able to establish a better relationship with his father and brother and to function as an *independent*, yet appropriately dependent, person.

CHAPTER 9

"Each Time I Shot One I Felt Better and Better"

The consequences of uncontrolled anger are the most devastating of the normal emotional reactions that occur in all human beings. The aggressiveness of man and animals has long been a subject of theoretical and experimental study, and numerous explanations for its appearance in individuals have been offered. One which most readers could easily understand is the so-called "frustration-aggression" hypothesis.

Simply stated, this theory holds that when an individual is striving to reach some goal or to obtain something he needs or wants, being stopped by something or someone from achieving his wishes will cause anger and aggressive behavior. For example, almost everyone has had the experience of trying to get someplace in a hurry and finding himself stuck behind a line of cars at a traffic light; a pretty normal response to this frustration is anger at various aspects of the situation. One person may use some choice words to describe the operation of the traffic lights, another may direct his invective at the drivers ahead of him. No matter how the person responds, however, the source of his anger in this situation is the blocking of his wishes.

Another explanation of how anger develops and is released may be found in social theory. Society, or the culture of which a person is a part, permits certain forms of anger and aggressive behavior and does not permit, or punishes, others. In our own American culture, anger may not be expressed directly very often; the person who is angry at another to the point where he wants to strike his antagonist is restrained by definite societal rules, such as laws of assault and battery, that effectively stop him.

American society does allow for certain other routes of expression. For example, many persons gain a great deal of satisfaction from watching prizefights or other forms of physically demanding and dangerous sports; for these persons, someone else is getting the beating and someone else is giving it, but watching the spectacle makes them feel less angry. It must be emphasized that this is a perfectly normal means of dealing with angry feelings.

Dealing with anger by violence, however, is not foreign to our society. There are certain groups or subcultures, that accept and encourage this mode of behavior. Thus, back in the days when gangs flourished in America, it was perfectly normal and acceptable for the gang leader to vent his anger by physically punishing a member of the gang subculture who had behaved inappropriately.

The basic point of this cultural explanation of aggressive behavior is that society defines those situations in which anger is an appropriate response and prescribes responses that are acceptable in the expression of the anger. If a society composed of murderers accepted murder as an appropriate interpersonal behavior for most of its members, murder would be considered a perfectly normal behavior.

The first example presented in this chapter deals with a person who was reared in a culture in which killing and violence were nonacceptable behaviors, but found himself the victim of a change in cultural direction. He is a twenty-two-year-old veteran of the Vietnam war who found that he was unable to accept and readjust to the requirements of a peacetime society after returning to the United States. He was unable to place limits on his aggression and anger and found himself at the brink of becoming involved with the law. He referred himself for psychotherapy when he found that he was angry all the time and was afraid that he would kill somebody if he did not obtain help.

Therapist. You seem to be a little calmer this week.

Client. Yes, I think that it's because I hope you'll be able to help me.

T. Good. Let's try to go back and trace the events that occurred when you first went to Vietnam.

C. Well . . . when I first got there I was really scared. I was in an infantry unit and I went out into the field about two weeks after I got there. Nothing happened for a while and I found that all I could think of was how I could never shoot anybody. You know what they say . . . only one out of four soldiers ever shoots at the enemy. Anyway, I was scared and couldn't stop thinking that if I couldn't shoot back, I'd be the one to get killed.

T. You must have been pretty tense waiting for something to happen.

C. I sure was . . . but it finally did. We were on a patrol up near the DMZ when we got ambushed. My first thought was "Oh, my God, this is it." My C.O. told us to rush the ambush and we did, but there must have been a hundred Viet Cong up there. We tried to hold them off, but we lost about half the patrol. Finally, the C.O. told us to get the hell out of there and we ran. I don't know how I kept running, but we got away.

T. Did you feel any different after that incident?

C. I started getting madder than I'd ever been. I lost one of my friends in that ambush and all I could think of was getting some of the V.C. to pay for that.

T. You weren't worried about killing people anymore?

C. Are you kidding? After what those fucking V.C. did to us? They weren't worth not shooting at.

T. I assume you got the chance to vent your anger.

C. Yeh, we went back to the field about a week later and before we knew it we ran into a bunch of V.C. We had them right where we wanted them and we tore 'em to shreds. Each time I shot one I felt better and better.

T. Your anger was being relieved?

C. Damn right. But the thing is that after two or three months of shooting those guys, I started doing it with no feeling at all. It was like, "Oh, there's one—Bang, bang, he's dead."

T. You became pretty callous about it.

C. Yeh, but that's what they wanted me to do I guess . . . I got promoted to full sergeant and got a bunch of medals for bravery.

T. So you spent your last few months in Vietnam killing without feeling bad about it. What happened when you came home?

C. Well, I was really glad to get the hell out of Nam. I came home . . . saw my girl and my family . . . everything was great for about two weeks.

T. What happened then?

C. I was over at my brother's house and we were having a friendly argument about something. I don't even remember what it was. Anyway, all of a sudden I got really mad . . . like I never was before I went to Nam. I jumped my brother and we were rolling on the floor. I don't know what happened for a few seconds, but when I realized what was happening I saw that I had him by the adam's apple and was ready to pull. If he weren't my brother I probably would have done it and killed him.

T. How did you feel after that happened?

C. I wasn't really upset . . . just mad . . . really mad. I left my brother's house and was driving home and I just got madder and madder.

T. How did you think you were going to deal with your anger?

C. I didn't have to think. As I was driving, two young punks and a girl cut me off. They turned around and I saw them laughing at me. That did it: I got in front of them and forced them to pull off the road. I got out and told them to get out of the car. As the first one leaned to get out, I kicked him right in the face and he fell back on the seat. I think I broke his nose. The other one came running around the car and jumped me from behind. I hit him one good one and he was down . . . he was through fighting, but I couldn't stop myself . . . I jumped on him and started pounding his face. The girl was screaming for help. It was the same feeling that I had with my brother . . . I didn't know what was happening . . . I couldn't stop.

T. Sounds frightening. How did you stop?

C.   The Highway Patrol came along and stopped us. I told him what happened and the girl in the other car said it was true. The cops let me go. I don't know what happened to those two guys, though. I poked them good.

T.   Did you feel less angry when you drove away?

C.   Yes, but I felt tense. I really didn't know myself.

T.   Did anything else happen?

C.   I got into more fights than I'd ever been in. No matter what people said to me I poked them. It seemed that I wanted them to say something to get me mad. All I wanted was an excuse to break somebody's face.

T.   Can you give me a specific example?

C.   Well, here's a strange one. I was at a party with my girl and this guy came up and started talking to her. He didn't mean anything I guess, but I got real mad. I told him to take off and leave her alone and he made some wisecrack. I would have smashed him right there if my girl hadn't pulled me away.

T.   So you controlled your anger.

C.   Hell, no. All I could think about for days after that was that guy and how he was probably thinking that I was a chicken. I couldn't get him out of my mind.

T.   What did you do?

C.   There was nothing I could do, but wait for my chance. I swore I'd get him. Anyway, about two weeks ago, I saw the dude downtown. He probably didn't even remember who I was, but I remembered him. I went up to him and didn't say a word. I caught him off guard and smashed his face. He just lay there on the ground looking up at me, but I really felt good.

T.   So your anger not only comes on inappropriately and rapidly, but it doesn't go away until you've hurt the guy who angered you?

C.   That's right.

T.   Have you tried releasing your feelings against things rather than people?

C.   Yeh, I tried hitting a wall, but I hurt my hand. Besides, a wall doesn't get hurt, and when I'm mad somebody has to be hurt.

T.   You can't get rid of your anger in ways other than physical violence in which you hurt other people?

C. Yeh, and if I try not to hit people right off, like you suggested a few weeks ago, I'm miserable.

T. How did you deal with your anger before you went to
Vietnam?

C. I didn't get angry then like I do now. Besides, I was
afraid I'd get smashed if I got into a fight. If anything,
Nam taught me that I could hurt people really well.

T. Before you mentioned that if you didn't hit a guy, then
he would think you were a chicken. Did you feel that
way before Vietnam?

C. Listen, before I went to Nam *I* thought I was a chicken.
I told you how scared I was when I first got there. I
proved to myself that I'm not and I'm not gonna let anybody else think that I am.

T. How do you know people think you're a chicken if you
don't hit them?

C. If I see a guy walk away from a fight *I* think he's a
chicken, so probably that's what other people think of
me when I walk away. Nobody's gonna think that about
me.

T. Apparently that's the way you're acting; you're trying
to show the world that you're not a person to get too
close to. But on another point . . . remember I asked
you not to hit the next guy you feel like hitting? How's
that been going?

C. Yeh, well I did that. A guy was talking to my girl in a
parking lot and I felt like going up to him and belting
him, but I didn't.

T. How do you feel about it?

C. I'm miserable, how do you think I feel? All I can think
about is that guy not getting hit when he should have.

T. Do you think that you're still going to get him?

C. Damn right. I have to . . . Do you know what I did
last night because of it?

T. What?

C. I sat home and fumed . . . all I could think about was
that guy not getting poked. I got mad at him and I got
mad at you for telling me not to hit the guy. I got so mad
I wound up getting my shoe and beating myself over the
head with it. I knocked myself down . . . craziest thing
I ever did. The only way I'll feel better is if I get that
guy.

T.   But that'll be hard to do. You only saw him in the parking lot.

C.   I found out where he lives and some morning I'll go there and when he comes out, pow.

Obviously, this client has a long way to go in psychotherapy. He has come back from Vietnam with the aggressive tools necessary to deal with many of the insecurities of his youth. Having been placed in a situation wherein direct violent expression of anger was encouraged and faced with an inability to discriminate between that situation and the one he is presently in have caused the client great difficulty. He reacted to the persons with whom he came into conflict in civilian life in the same way as he reacted to his opponents in war. Luckily, he had enough ego strength to stop himself before he killed his brother and some of the others with whom he fought.

Through the process of psychotherapy, this client's inability to control his anger and aggression was explored, and the interesting fact that he turned against himself when completely blocked from expression was dealt with in depth. Even after lengthy psychotherapy, however, he was not again totally able to reintegrate himself into a culture in which free and open expression of anger through violent means is discouraged. Were he to have remained in Vietnam or to have returned to a culture more tolerant of such behavior, he probably would not have experienced the intense emotional discomfort that led him to seek treatment.

While the uncontrolled expression of anger and aggression creates problems for both society as well as the individual involved, the overcontrol of anger has more of an effect on the individual alone. The person who, for one reason or another, does not allow his anger to be expressed, but who keeps it locked tightly inside of him at all times, falls into this category of problems. The necessity of controlling so much anger often requires a great deal of psychological energy, resulting in a less than optimal level of individual functioning; this overcontrol also causes much anxiety about the possibility that controls will break down and the anger will come out in a devastating flood.

The cause of overcontrol of emotion is a theoretical question, but certain plausible explanations can be offered. Take, for example, the childhood situation in which parents will not tolerate any anger expressed towards them. Of course in a child's life parents are one of the main sources of frustrated desires. They are the ones who say "no new toys"; they do the disciplining. Anger is the child's normal reaction to many parental actions. In most families, the child is allowed to vent his anger in some safe, indirect way, but there are situations in which any expression of anger is met with severe punishment. The adult who has been raised in such a repressive atmosphere may find that he is unable to express his anger to anyone, especially those in authority. (And these are the main sources of frustration for adults.) Thus, through childhood experiences, a person whose aggressive behavior has been overcontrolled may be very anxious not to say he is angry and fear the thought that his anger might vent itself. In the same way, when such a person finally expresses his anger, the result is more damaging than if it had been expressed in small, relevant amounts.

The result of such repression is exemplified by a twenty-eight-year-old woman who has been married for six years and is the mother of a three-year-old boy. She referred herself for psychotherapy because she was "tense all day, every day" and was unable to function as she thought a wife and mother should. During the initial interview, it was determined that she had been rather strictly supervised during childhood and her parents had never allowed her to express anger at them. Furthermore, when she kicked doors or threw tantrums as indirect expressions of her feelings, her behavior was met with severe punishment.

Client.   Doctor, I've been thinking all week about our discussions about my childhood. I don't think my parents hated me. Why do you think they treated me as they did?
Therapist.   Apparently you haven't been able to come up with a good answer to that question, so you're asking

me. But I'd like to know what possibilities you've thought about.

C. Well, when I look at me as a parent and when I look back at them, the only answer I get is that they were pretty insecure about being parents and that when I became angry with them, they thought it was an indication that they weren't doing a good job.

T. I think that's a plausible explanation. Did you think of any others?

C. Only the same ones that I thought about when I was a teenager . . . that for some reason they didn't want me to bother them.

T. How does that thought make you feel?

C. Not too good. . . . In a way I'd rather believe that they were insecure parents.

T. You mentioned that you were comparing them as parents to yourself. How does that fit in?

C. Well, I think that I don't show Bobby that I'm really mad at him because I'm afraid that he'll get mad at me . . . and if he does . . . well, then I think I'll take it as meaning he doesn't like me as a parent.

T. Its hard to see how you got to that point in your thinking, but I think what you're saying is that you're afraid to yell at him and be rejected by him.

C. Right . . . and that's the same way I dealt with my parents. That's kind of funny . . . here I am, a parent, dealing with my child as if *he* were the parent.

T. Does your fear of being angry or showing anger affect your relationship with your husband?

C. No, he rarely gives me reason to be angry.

T. I find that pretty hard to believe. You're telling me that in six years of marriage, you haven't even become angry at him once?

C. Well . . . I guess I do get angry at him sometimes.

T. When was the last time?

C. Let me see. . . . Oh . . . I know, it was about a month ago. I'd been asking him for quite a while to take Bobby and me on a vacation and he kept saying that he had too much work to do and wouldn't be able to for a long time.

T. What did you feel when he said that?

C. I felt like telling him that Bobby and I never get to go anywhere and that he should think of us now and then instead of his job.

T. But you didn't tell him that.

C. No, of course not. I told him that I hope he can get his work up to date so that we could go.

T. Did that make you feel better?

C. It made me feel differently. . . . I mean . . . I didn't feel really angry. I just felt sorry for Bobby because we couldn't get away for a trip. He would have enjoyed it.

T. Both of you children would have.

C. What do you mean?

T. Well, before you said that you told your husband that Bobby and you would like to go on a trip. That was like saying that the children in the family are asking Daddy to take them someplace. Then you said that your anger turned to feeling sorry for Bobby. Again, you were reacting like a child who did not get her way and was feeling bad. But instead of feeling bad directly, you placed the feelings upon your son.

C. Yes, I can see your point, but how does that help things? I think I've been acting like that with my husband as long as we've been married.

T. What would happen if you really told your husband that you were angry?

C. I don't know.

T. Try to imagine it.

C. O.K. . . . I guess he'd get angry back at me.

T. O.K. so he would show you anger back and you're afraid of people becoming angry at you.

C. Yes, well, I don't really know how to deal with that. My first reaction is to get even madder, but that would probably bring more on me.

T. All right, what would happen if you got really mad at him and he got really mad at you?

C. We'd end up in a big fight and I may say things I don't really mean. And he'd probably say things too.

T. I don't know if you wouldn't mean what you would say. You'd probably say things that you've kept inside yourself for a long time and you're probably afraid that they'll destroy your relationship with your husband.

C. That's true . . . and if I've got things like that to say, imagine what he would say.

T. So you feel that there are a lot of dissatisfactions he has that he's not telling you . . . you probably don't want to hear them, so you're avoiding a confrontation in which they'll come out.

C. Yes . . . sure.

T. O.K., what will happen if they come out?

C. What do you mean? Do you mean will we get a divorce? I don't know.

T. You went right from a big fight to a divorce . . . to complete rejection of you by your husband. The rejection for being angry seems to be the thing you fear most.

C. Now that we talk about it, I guess that's right.

T. Yes, and like it was with you and your parents, if you show your anger, he would reject you . . . not like you.

C. Yes, it is like it was with my parents, but how can I show my husband I'm angry?

The client has now come to realize that most of her difficulties with the expression of anger stem from her childhood experiences. Knowing this fact, however, does not really help her to deal with her husband in the present. The interview was important in other ways, however, for it gave her a reason to see that things could be different now. She could see that she did not have a good method of communicating her feelings to her husband and that her fear of his rejection made it impossible for her to be happy.

As mentioned, however, this did not help her to deal with her husband. To achieve this goal, therapy became more directed at the present and less to the past. She was encouraged, with her husband's knowledge and cooperation, to experiment with the expression of anger. She was guided into appropriate and nondangerous (for her) ways of saying she was mad about things. She overcame her fear that her husband would reject her when she realized that he, too, was uncomfortable in the marriage because he was never confident that she was being honest with him (which she was not). This client was able to overcome her overcontrol of anger through the experience of psychotherapy and the insight and direction it gave her. At last report, she is quite happy, and her marriage is stable and secure.

CHAPTER 10

"I Was So Scared I Couldn't Move"

Fear is no stranger to anyone. We all have fears that interfere with our lives to a greater or lesser degree. However, some individuals have fears that are so strong and interfere with their lives to such a great degree that they need the help of a psychotherapist. Some of these individuals have been called phobics, a term that refers to individuals who have a morbid dread of an object or situation that does not evoke such a response from most people.

Intense fears may be attached to a remarkable variety of objects or situations, ranging from animals, such as snakes and insects, to situations, such as closed-in spaces, extreme heights, high speeds, and being outside of one's house. There is virtually no limit to the type of situation that may evoke an individual's fear.

It should be noted that psychotherapists attribute fear of a given object or situation to many different causes. Some view fears as symbols that relate to a more deep-seated psychological fear, while others believe that fears have only minimal symbolic significance. Psychotherapists who believe that fear is a symptom probably will be interested in exploring a client's background to discern the basis of the aversion symbolized by the fear. Presumably, when the real problem is found, the symbolic fear will disappear. Psychotherapists who believe that fear has only minimal symbolic significance, however, are more inclined to treat the fear about which the client complains directly, aiming for a goal of immediate symptomatic relief. Proponents of this latter position, who often call themselves "behavior therapists" or "behavior modifiers," have developed several approaches that seem to have fairly rapid ameliorating effects on fears.

We will illustrate some approaches now. While it may seem that the therapist is treating the client passively, as though a doctor can cure his patient, this is not the case. As mentioned in Chapter 1, the psychotherapist cannot "fix" a client's problem. The ultimate change in behavior must come from the client. The techniques that have been developed from the behavior modification point of view can be effective only if the clients to whom they are applied are truly motivated to overcome their fears.

Before illustrating the treatment techniques, a general consideration regarding the psychotherapeutic treatment of fears must be discussed. This consideration is not new to the reader, for it has been repeated in virtually every chapter of this book. In the clearest way possible, the client with extremely severe fears in psychotherapy must tell the psychotherapist the situations that evoke the fears and the situations that terminate them as well as the thoughts and feelings that accompany the fears. This "patterning" information is vital to the psychotherapist if he is to help his client with the development of a treatment plan.

The first interview in the chapter illustrates a client's sincere attempt to present the "patterning" of his fear to a psychotherapist:

Client.   Well, it's like . . . well, every time I have to ride in an elevator, I just get this panicky feeling, like . . . well, I can't really describe it very well. I just get this panicky feeling, like I have to get out of there fast, or I'll go out of my mind. I can't really remember when it first started. I do remember getting so scared once that I started screaming, and I ran off of the elevator as soon as it got to the next floor. Everyone looked at me like I was crazy, but I couldn't help it. I guess I was more frightened than embarrassed. I just couldn't stand it.

Therapist.   You say that you can't recall when it started?

C.   Not really, although I know it must've been a long time
ago. For a long time, I avoided elevators and took the
stairs, but the way they're building office buildings these
days, I'd have to walk up twenty or thirty flights of
stairs to get where I want to go, and then I'm so tired
and perspired that I can't bring myself to see the people
I have to see. I'm a salesman, you know, and I just
can't crawl into one of my client's offices, panting away
and sweating from climbing thirty flights of stairs, and
expect to make a very good impression. That's why I
came to see you. My sales have been dropping, and if I
want to make a living, I'm going to have to get over this
thing. Lately, like this last time, I tried getting mad at
myself. I mean, all these people ride elevators every day,
and it doesn't bother them, so I just get mad at myself,
and grit my teeth, and say that it won't bother me. But
it's not easy to do. The last time, I really got all psyched
up for it, and I was determined that come what may, I
wasn't going to get off that elevator until it got to my
floor. Well, as I got to the building, I started to panic.
It's a cold feeling, sort of, like in the pit of your stomach,
and you feel so helpless, like something terrible's going
to happen, and there's nothing you can do about it. Well,
I was determined anyway, like I said, but the feeling got
stronger and stronger and I got into the building and
walked toward the elevator. I was still determined, but
when that elevator door opened, and I looked in, I just
couldn't do it. I couldn't go in. So I walked up ten flights
of stairs and waited in the men's room until I caught
my breath before I went in to see the customer. I've just
got to get over this. It's either that, or find a new job, I
guess.

T.   What happened to the feeling of panic when you finally
decided not to enter the elevator or, on those occasions
when you did get in, what happened to the feeling of
panic when you got out?

C.   Well, it goes away pretty quickly. As soon as I walk
away from it, the feeling goes away.

T.   Was there any other time in your life when you got a
feeling like the one you describe when you get near an
elevator?

C. No, I don't think so. It's only when I have to ride in an elevator.

T. What about when you have to ride in an elevator to see someone other than a customer?

C. That doesn't seem to make any difference. As long as it's an elevator, I get panicked. It doesn't happen any other time. Like, I can be packed into a car with other people, and that doesn't bother me, and I don't think that it's the height of a building that bothers me, because I can walk up to the top of a building and look down out of a window, and that won't bother me either.

T. Do you have any thoughts about what it is that makes elevators so frightening to you?

C. (Silence). No, I really can't think of any reason why I should be so panicked about elevators. I mean, I've never been in an accident in an elevator, and I don't think I know of anyone else who's been in one. There's no one that I know who's afraid of them. I just don't know why I should be this way.

The client in the above excerpt has made a fairly clear presentation of the important aspects of his fear. He has told the therapist how the fear begins, how it ends, how he feels when he is confronted with the situation and is not afraid, and, to the best of his knowledge, that he has not learned the fear from anyone else. It may be that the fear of riding in elevators is a symbol of an underlying fear—perhaps of being shut into a small space and suffocating. On the other hand, it may be that the fear is simply a fear of elevators that he has learned over a long period of time. It is not necessarily true that a fear is learned from one traumatic incident. Rather, a fear may be acquired slowly, in a manner similar to the way in which one learns a poem, without the occurrence of any one outstanding experience.

The exact nature of the client's fear can be determined only after an examination and exploration of other spheres of the client's life. If the therapist believes that the client's fear is simply a straightforward fear of elevators, he might deal with it by employing either behavior modifiers, systematic desensitization, *in vivo* desensitization, or implosive therapy.

Systematic desensitization relies on the assumption that a fear can be inhibited by enabling the client to be in the feared situation while behaving in a manner that is incompatible with being afraid. The procedure begins with the view that one cannot be afraid and relaxed at the same time; that if the client can be helped to relax in the feared situation, he will not be afraid. The client is first instructed in the art of relaxation to achieve a low level of nervous tension. He is then asked to construct a hierarchy of feared situations, with the aid of the therapist, going from the least fearful to the most fearful.

Using the individual who is afraid of riding in an elevator, a hierarchy of feared situations might look like this:

1. Walking along the street with no plans to ride in an elevator.
2. Knowing that you must visit a customer whose office is on the thirtieth floor of a building.
3. Knowing that you must visit this customer immediately.
4. Thinking that you must ride in an elevator if you are to see the customer.
5. Approaching the building with the thought of riding in the elevator.
6. Walking into the building.
7. Approaching the elevator.
8. Opening of the elevator doors.
9. Stepping into the elevator.
10. Closing the elevator doors behind you.
11. Starting to ascend in the elevator.
12. Getting stuck between floors for a long period of time.
13. Experiencing the sensation that the elevator cables have broken and you are falling to your death.

In the above hierarchy, the least feared situation is presented first and the most feared situation last. The client who is in a deeply relaxed state is asked to imagine the first scene on the hierarchy while he concentrates on being relaxed. If the client feels anxiety or fear, he signals the therapist, who then asks the client to stop imagining the scene and to concentrate on the relaxation. The scene is then reintroduced.

This process goes on until the client can imagine the scene without feeling any anxiety or fear. At this time, the second scene on the hierarchy is introduced, and the process continues until the client can imagine each scene on the hierarchy without experiencing discomfort. The client is then encouraged to go out and approach an elevator until he feels anxious, to concentrate on relaxing and, at the same time, to move nearer to the elevator.

In a systematic desensitization, the client must imagine the scenes so vividly that he experiences the fear that would occur if he were actually living the scenes in real life. Only if he can do this successfully will the procedure have a rapid effect. Further, he must report to the therapist any thoughts or feelings he has while imagining himself in the feared situation, as such reports may provide further information about the nature of the fear.

A variation of the systematic desensitization, called *in vivo* desensitization, may be used with a client who is unable to imagine feared scenes vividly enough to feel the fear and anxiety he would feel if he were actually in the situation. This procedure, which is based on the same principles as systematic desensitization, is performed in much the same way, but it is carried out in real life. Thus, the therapist would accompany the client who is afraid of elevators to a building that had an elevator. As they approached the elevator the therapist would instruct the client to relax. As the client's anxiety increased, they would move away from the elevator until the anxiety dissipated, at which point they would approach the elevator again. Again, as in systematic desensitization, the client must practice relaxation on his own and report to the psychotherapist any particular thoughts or ideas that he might experience during the treatment procedure.

Implosive therapy is a third method of treating fear. The principle behind implosive therapy is somewhat different from that used in systematic desensitization. In desensitization procedures, the therapist attempts to combat fears by inducing the client to relax. In implosive therapy, however, he assumes that the type of fear that troubles individuals stays with them because they have never remained in the feared situation long enough to realize that their fears are unwarranted. They avoid the feared situation and can never be sure that their fears are not justified. For example, the client with the elevator phobia has never been able to ride an elevator—he has always tried to escape the situation. This escape keeps him from realizing that he can ride the elevator to his destination without any terrible consequences.

An analogue to implosive therapy might be viewed this way: imagine that we are trying to teach a pet dog that he is never to sit on a particular piece of furniture in a home. Let us assume that we teach him not to sit on this piece of furniture by placing him on it and then hitting him with a piece of newspaper. We only stop hitting him when he jumps off of the furniture. Once he has learned this, he will leap off of the furniture as soon as he is placed there—he will not go near it.

Let us assume that we have changed our minds and want the dog to know that it is now permissible to sit on the piece of furniture. How do we accomplish this task? It seems very difficult. If we place the dog on the furniture and tell him to stay, the strength of his fear will impel him to leap off immediately. He will not stay long enough to realize that he will not be punished. The problem can be solved if we can find a way to force the dog to stay on the furniture—to set up a situation that he cannot escape. He will be terrified for a while, of course, but, if we keep him there long enough, and repeat the procedure often enough, he will slowly learn that he will not be punished for sitting on the furniture, and the fear will disappear.

The problem faced in treating the fearful human being is not much different. Humans may learn to be afraid of situations in a variety of ways but, like the dog, once they learn the fear, they never stay in the feared situation long enough to realize that their fears are not justified and that they won't be harmed.

Implosive therapy works with humans the way keeping the dog on the furniture works with the dog. The fearful individual is instructed to imagine that he is in the feared situation and his worst fears about that situation are, in fact, confirmed. He is instructed to hold this image for a long period of time, and not to allow himself to escape by putting the feared thoughts out of his mind. This procedure is continued until the client shows some sign of decreasing anxiety, at which point he is reassured that his fears were not really confirmed, and that he is safe. It may be necessary to repeat the procedure, but as a result, the client will become much less afraid and more able to function adequately in the feared situation.

To illustrate a variation in the implosive therapy procedure, we will present an excerpt of an interview with a young married woman who has an overwhelming fear of earthquakes. She has never been in an earthquake, nor does she know anyone who has. Yet, almost every night, she is awakened by the fear that an earthquake will strike. On several occasions, she has arisen from bed, picked up her son, and run to the doorway of her house, waiting for the earthquake to start. Her difficulty with sleeping has made her tired and irritable much of the time and, in general, has had a major destructive effect on her life. When discussing her fear, she mentioned that when she begins to think about the earthquake, she always imagines the same thing happening until she becomes so frightened that she must "put it out of my mind and think of something else." This clearly illustrates the fact that she "escapes" the feared situation rather than sticking with it and learning that she need not be so frightened.

Therapist.   Now I want you to begin thinking about being in an earthquake the way you do at home, only I don't want you to put the thoughts out of your mind the way you usually do. This time, I want you to keep thinking about the earthquake as if it is really happening, and tell me what your thoughts are and what images you see. Close your eyes and begin.

Client.   O.K. Well, it's late at night, and I'm beginning to get scared. It's dark out, and I'm worried that there's going to be an earthquake. I'm lying in bed, and I'm just so scared that I can't move. (The client begins to squirm in her seat, and perspiration appears on her forehead.) I'm thinking about what I'm going to do when the earthquake hits—about my baby—I've got to get to my baby. Now I think that I can feel the ground starting to shake, and it's frightening. The ground is rumbling and the house is creaking, and I just know that it's going to collapse right on top of me. I'm shaking all over (the client's body begins to tremble), and I feel this cold feeling coming over me, like I'm going to die. I can't stand it any more (silence).

T. The ground is shaking furiously, and you're so scared that you can't move. The house is starting to collapse, and you're terrified. Go on. What's happening now? Don't stop. Keep going.

C. I . . . I can't . . . I can't stand it anymore. My baby (beginning to cry), my baby, I have to get my baby. I have to get to him before the house falls on him. I've got to get to him.

T. Go on. You've got to get your baby. The house is starting to collapse and it's going to crush him. What's happening now? Keep going.

C. I've got to get to him (sobbing). I have to get him out. I'm getting up out of bed and I'm running into his room, and the house is starting to go. I have to reach him. I go running up to him, and he's crying. He's so scared, and I have him now, and I'm running to the doorway of the house—that's the only safe place I can think of. I have to get him to safety. The house is falling now. I can't . . . I can't stand it anymore (crying and sobbing). I can't go on. I can't.

T. Yes, you can. You must. Force yourself. What's happening now? What's going on? Stay with it, fight it. Don't put it out of your mind. You're in the doorway of the house with the baby, and the house is collapsing around you. What's happening now?

C. The house is coming down all around me . . . oh, I can't.

T. You must. You have to. What's next?

C. The house, it's falling. The boards are falling all around me, and I'm holding my baby (screaming). Oh, my God, stop it! Stop it! I can't stand it!

T. No. You have to keep going. What's happening now?

The boards are falling all around you. What's happening now?

C.   Ahh! I'm hit by a board, and it falls on top of me. The ground is shaking, and it sounds like the end of the world. Oh, no! I can't get out from under the board. It's so heavy. I can't move it. My baby, where's my baby? He's trapped under the board, too. The dust is so thick I can hardly breathe. I'm suffocating! I can't breathe. The board is laying right across my chest, and I can't breathe . . . Scream . . . scream for help. I have to scream for help. Help! Help! Please, won't somebody help me? Oh, my God, I'm going to die. Please, somebody, anybody! Help me! (Crying) . . . Oh, I can't . . . I can't do any more. Please, I can't.

T.   Keep going! Stay with it. What's happening now? Don't stop. Keep going!

C.   There's nobody to help me. Nobody's coming to help. They can't hear me. The ground's making too much noise. The rumbling, the baby's crying because he can't breathe. I can't move. The board has me pinned down and I can't move at all. Oh, please, please, somebody help me! (Sobbing) . . . Oh . . . I can't fight anymore . . . let me die. Let me go . . . I can't move this board. Oh, if only I could move the board . . . wait! Wait! The ground . . . it's stopping . . . my God, my dear sweet Jesus . . . it's stopping, oh my God, it's stopping.

T.   The earthquake is stopping. The ground isn't rumbling anymore. Now what's happening?

C.   I'm screaming. Help! Help me! Somebody help me please . . . get this board off of me. I can't breathe. My baby, my baby can't breathe. Please, please somebody help us. We're trapped. Trapped . . . I'm screaming for help, but nobody's coming. It's . . . it's getting light. I must have been trapped this way for hours. It's morning, and I'm still screaming, but I have nothing left to scream with. My voice is all gone, and I can't scream anymore. Look, what's happening? The boards are moving. I can move the boards around. If I can only move this one. Oh, God, give me the strength to move this one. (Straining) I . . . I'm moving it a little. Oh, look, I'm moving it. Oh, I can breathe, I can breathe.

(Laughing and crying) I can breathe again. My baby. My baby's alive. He's alive. Oh, dear God, he's alive. Now I've got him, and I'm standing up. My back hurts, and my ribs hurt, but I'm standing up. I'm walking away. I'm walking away from it. The sun's out, and I can breathe. (Takes a deep breath and sinks down into the chair, weeping and exhausted.)

After several sessions similar to the one above, the client was no longer troubled by her fear of earthquakes. It should be noted that the above excerpt illustrated a variation of implosive therapy—the client provided the content of the imagery. A more usual procedure involves the therapist telling the client what to imagine.

It might seem to the reader that in the excerpt presented above, the client was extremely frightened and the therapist was cruel to use such a procedure. Even though the client was very upset and frightened, the procedure has been shown to be effective; it seems much less cruel to help a client get over a fear than to let the fear dominate his life.

When viewing the three forms of treatment presented in this chapter, it is extremely important to recognize that all procedures involve helping the client to actually experience the feared situation. This common attribute reflects the fact that while the therapist who uses these techniques may be very active and directive in telling the client what to do, it is still the client who must face his fears. These techniques may make the task a bit easier for the client, but by no means do they alter his responsibility of working to achieve his successful treatment.

CHAPTER 11

"Why Do I Let People Walk All Over Me?"

Discomfort, a fear related to those discussed in Chapter 10, is experienced by many individuals in the interactions that call for assertiveness—the ability to stand up for oneself. Difficulties in assertiveness may stem from such sources as overbearing parents, physical weakness, lack of experience in situations calling for assertive behavior, and confusion between aggressiveness and assertive behavior.

This last factor, confusing assertion and aggression, is quite common. Many people feel that assertive and aggressive behavior are synonymous. Consequently, they are reluctant to behave assertively. They fear that others will also see aggressiveness in assertive behavior and therefore wish to retaliate in kind. This fear of retaliation is one of the strongest factors that inhibit self-assertion.

Lack of assertiveness that is partially attributable to a fear of retaliation may occur in many different contexts, but often, individuals who experience such difficulties seem to find perfectly good reasons for their reluctance to stand up for themselves. Certainly, they argue, a demanding boss can fire an employee who asserts himself, and a merchant who is confronted by an angry customer can deny a service. One must take what comes and not argue too intensely, or one can get hurt.

More often than not, such arguments are simply means of justifying the reluctance that many people feel when faced with the necessity of speaking up for themselves.

These individuals often feel they are being slighted but are unable to do anything about it. They may become extremely angry but never express their anger to anyone who can hurt them. Instead, they may take their feelings out on others who are not in a position to retaliate. A common example of this kind of behavior is the junior executive who has a bad day at the office, comes home, and kicks the cat.

Unfortunately, the indirect release of anger may not be nearly as effective as a direct expression of self-assertion for two reasons. First, the expression of anger can only be beneficial if that expression removes or changes the situation that created the anger in the first place. Thus, kicking the cat is of little help since it has nothing to do with what made the executive angry in the first place. He still must face his boss, and if it is his boss who makes him angry, the source of the anger will not be affected in the least by whatever he does to the cat. Second, the individual who expresses his anger indirectly is likely to experience some loss of self-respect after "punishing" some irrelevant object. He realizes that the object is not making him angry and becomes even more self-critical. Determining whether anger should be expressed directly or indirectly is of secondary importance, however. The real issue is that assertive behavior, when expressed appropriately, often reduces the need for anger or aggression. Assertion is not the same as aggression and need not produce the same reaction from other people. On the contrary, assertiveness elicits the respect of others as well as enhances the individual's own self-respect.

Some persons frequently experience difficulty in acting assertively; for others, this difficulty may present a problem only in certain special circumstances. The psychotherapy client who experiences difficulties with assertive behavior must first try to clarify the situations in which he finds it most difficult to assert himself. The description should include those aspects of the situation that bring on the difficulty as well as what happens after the situation has passed. The first interview in this chapter illustrates one client's attempt to describe the pattern of his difficulties with self-assertion.

Client. Sometimes I get so mad at myself for not saying anything to him . . . my boss, I mean. For Christ's sake, who does he think I am, his pet dog? The way he orders me around, you'd think I had long ears and a tail. Do this, do that, hurry up, take care of this, do it now. That's the way it is from the time I get to work to the time I leave, when I leave. There are times when he'll walk in at about 4:45 and ask me to do something that keeps me there until after 6:00 o'clock. I don't know what to say. I mean, I have my own life to lead. I have a wife and a family, and I want to be with them. I never signed a blood pact to devote my entire life to that place. I want to be able to get to work at 9:00 o'clock and leave at 5:00; I don't want to worry about staying late or anything like that. It's just not fair that it's always me that he picks on. There are plenty of others who could do the same thing. But no—it's always me. That's the way it always was, too. Not just at this job. All of the jobs I've ever had have been like that. There are always plenty of people around, but I'm the one who gets asked to stay late, or to do an extra project, or to come in on a weekend. Why do I let people walk all over me?

Therapist. Have you ever tried to tell any of your bosses that you can't always stay late when they ask you?

C. Tell them that I won't stay late? Are you kidding? That's the quickest way I know of to get canned. They don't have to put up with that stuff from me. I mean, they're bosses, and I just do a small nothing kind of a job. It wouldn't do me any good to just up and refuse. That'd be like asking to get fired.

T. Have you ever seen anyone else refuse a request on the part of a boss?

C. Well, let's see . . . yeah, I think I remember once when this other guy said that he couldn't stay because he had something else to do. Boy, I thought he was crazy. I could never do anything like that.

T. Why not? What stops you?

C. I don't know. I mean, the boss says to do something, and you do it, if you want your job. And besides, they give you that look, like you'd better cooperate if you know what's good for you. I just tremble in my shoes when I get that look. I know it sounds dumb, but I just get paralyzed and do whatever I'm told to do. (Laughs) I guess I'd almost jump off a bridge if I had to. I just get scared. My poor wife, she's the one who takes the brunt of it. I have to call her and tell her that I may not be home in time for dinner, and she has to run around like mad trying to fix things so that I'll have something to eat when I get home, and by the time I get home, I'm so upset and angry that I can't eat anyway.

T. So, in a way, you wind up taking it out at home.

C. Yeah, I sure do. It's not just not being able to eat, either. I know that it's not right, but after one of these episodes at work, I'm just unfit to be around. My kids know by now that they'd better be out of the way when I get home or there'll be hell to pay. I pace back and forth like a caged lion, sometimes for a couple of hours. Sometimes, I even go out for a long walk to get it all out of my system and the next morning, when I go back to work, I want to hide. It takes a day or two for me to get it out of my system.

T. Who else has there been in your life that you couldn't stand up to?

C. Who else? I guess there's been lots of others. I mean, I never could stand up to my teachers, for one thing. I'd always be the one to do the dirty jobs that other kids refused to do. Well, wait a minute . . . it's not that the other kids refused to do them. I don't even remember them being asked to do them. It seems to me like I was always picked for some reason. It makes me so mad . . . but I never knew what to do about it.

In psychotherapy, the interview itself is often used to establish information regarding the way in which a client's difficulties in assertiveness manifest themselves. This may be done in a variety of ways. Client and therapist may assume "roles" and enact scenes that the client reports as difficult for him to deal with. This role-playing enables the therapist to get a firsthand picture of the way in which the client handles himself in situations calling for assertive behavior. Role-playing is also advantageous when the therapist assumes the role of the client. In this way, the client has an opportunity to witness an example of assertiveness that he can then try to copy or use as a model. A third advantage of role-playing is that a relatively permissive and comfortable therapeutic relationship is established in which the client can practice being assertive without fearing that the therapist will retaliate. By providing feedback information regarding the effectiveness of the client's assertive behavior, the therapist can help his client learn to be more assertive in daily life.

The next excerpt illustrates the use of role-playing as a means of exploring situations that call for assertive behavior and the client's response in such situations, as well as providing an assertive "model" that the client can attempt to imitate. The client is the same person interviewed in the chapter's first excerpt above.

Therapist.   In order to help me get a clear picture of what's been happening with you at work, why don't you try and describe the most recent incident with your boss.

Client.   Well, let's see . . . it was about a week ago. It was on a Friday afternoon, and I was trying to finish up my work so that I'd have nothing hanging over my head over the weekend. I like to be able to get my week's work done by the end of the week, because it's awful to come to work on Monday morning and still have last week's work to finish up. Anyway, I was getting the last of my work finished, and the boss came in, threw a load of orders on my desk and said that they had to be done before Monday. I guess you can imagine how I felt. I mean, there was no way that I could get them done before I left that night, which meant that I'd have to come in on the weekend. But I had plans to go away for a quick trip with my wife over the weekend, and this just killed everything. I was lucky that my wife was so understanding about it. We just put off the trip, but I could tell that she was pretty upset.

T.   How did you react when your boss gave you all that extra work to do?

C.   How did I react? Well, I tried to let him know that it was a bad weekend for me to have to do extra work, but I gave in, of course. I mean, what else could I do?

T.   You say that you tried to let him know that it was a bad weekend for you to have extra work. How did you try to let him know?

C.   Well, I . . . I . . . well, I guess I sort of gave him a look like "please, not this weekend," but I guess he didn't catch it.

T.   But you didn't actually say anything to him.

C.   No, I really didn't say anything. I just sort of looked at him but it didn't do any good.

T.   I tell you what. Why don't we act out the scene as it happened. That'll really help me to get a handle on what it is that you did in the situation, and maybe we can work out something to help you out when circumstances like this arise again.

C.   Act out the scene? I'm afraid I'm not sure what you mean.

T.   I'll play the part of your boss, and you play yourself. We'll pretend that this is the real thing. Try not to break role, and try as hard as you can to feel that I am your boss, and that this is the real thing, O.K.?

C.   Fine. I'll give it a try.

T.   O.K. I'm your boss, and I walk into your office with a load of work, and I say, Look, we've got a pile of orders here that just have to get out before Monday. Please take care of it.

C.   Well, I . . . uh . . . O.K., I guess. Will it take much time? I mean, it's O.K., but, I mean, will it take too long to do today?

T.   Probably be too much to be done today. Just so you get it out before Monday. That's all that matters. You can come in over the weekend.

C.   But I . . . well . . . O.K., if it's that important.

T.   O.K., now let's break role for a second and talk about what just happened. Was this fairly close to what actually did happen between you and your boss?

C.   Yes, it was pretty much that way. But what else could I have done? I mean, it was important to get that stuff out and all, and I just didn't see any way out.

T.   All right, now let me ask you how you felt during this bit of role-playing. We'll get to the issue of other ways to handle it in a minute.

C.   How did I feel? I guess I felt upset—yes, upset, and I guess, a little angry.

T. Angry?

C. Yes, I was angry. I mean, I felt angry. Wouldn't you feel angry if that happened to you?

T. Yes, I suppose I would've felt angry too, but I didn't see any anger from you.

C. I guess I keep it pretty well hidden.

T. What would happen if you were to let it out a little?

C. Hell, I couldn't do that. I mean, I'd get fired if I let it out in this situation.

T. Maybe that would happen if you let it all out, but I doubt that it would happen if you let it out just a little bit. What I'm getting at is that I think it would be better to be a little assertive rather than angry a lot.

C. Yes, I suppose that would be good, but I have no idea how to do it.

T. Well, let's go back to the scene we just acted out. What other ways might there be to handle it?

C. I suppose I could've told him to get lost, but that would mean that I could pick up my last paycheck.

T. Yes, telling him to get lost is too harsh, but isn't there something else—something in between telling him to get lost and not being able to tell him anything?

C. There probably is, but I really don't know what else I could say, unless I pleaded with him to let me off because I had plans with my wife. But I can't beg like that. I mean, how can any self-respecting guy beg like that?

T. I'm not suggesting that you beg, but I wonder if you see any way in which you could've used the information about your plans in an assertive way with your boss— a way that wouldn't be begging.

C. (Silence) I . . . I suppose I could've told him that I had other plans. Is that what you mean?

T. That's getting there.

C. But how can you tell your boss that you have other plans —just like that? I mean, he'd never accept that.

T. I think that there might be a way to tell him that he would accept. Why don't we play out the scene again, only this time, let me play your part, and you be the boss.

C. O.K. Well, I come into the office with all those orders and put them on the desk, and I say, Let's get these out before Monday, O.K.?

T. Well, I have plans with my wife to go away for the

weekend, and, since we've had these plans for so long, I'm not sure I could break them so easily.

C.   Look, I'm not all that concerned about your weekend plans. Now, I'm sorry, but we have to get these orders out. There's no two ways about it.

T.   Well, isn't there anyone else around who could handle it? We have had these plans for such a long time. It would be quite costly for me to have to cancel them now.

C.   Well, I really haven't checked with anyone else yet. You've never let me down before.

T.   I know, and that's why I thought that maybe this time you'd ask someone else. I'm always putting in extra time, and this one time is very important to me.

C.   Well, I don't know . . .

T.   I tell you what. There are a few other guys around who know how to make up these orders. If we split them up between us, we'd probably be able to get them done before closing today. Then they'd be taken care of and no one would have to put in any extra time.

C.   Hey, that's a good idea. Why didn't I ever think of that before?

T.   Well, that's only one way to try and work around the problem. Now that we've broken our roles, maybe you could tell me how you felt about this last enactment.

C.   Well, it sounded really good. I don't know if I could've said it like that, but it seems like a reasonable way to handle this kind of thing. I really don't think that I could've done it, though.

T.   All right, why don't we switch roles again. I'll be the boss and you be you and try to do the best you can—try to be a little assertive.

C.   O.K.

T.   Look, we've just gotten in some new orders and they have to be out by Monday morning. Will you take care of them please?

C.   Yes, well, uh, you see, I've got these plans to go away with my wife for the weekend, and it would be kind of hard for us to cancel out now.

T.   I'm really sorry, but these orders just won't wait. We have to get them out right away. I'm sure your wife will understand.

C.   It's not as simple as that. I mean, under normal conditions, you know that I'd be glad to do it for you. It's just that we've had these plans for so long, and we've put money down already, and it'd be a financial loss as well as a disappointment to us to have to cancel.

T. Well, again I'm sorry, but I just don't see any other way. You'll have to get them done before Monday. There's nothing I can do about it.

C. Have you checked with any of the others to see if one of them can do it?

T. No, I haven't, and I didn't think I'd have to. You've never let me down before. What's gotten into you?

C. Nothing, really, I mean, well . . . look. Let me ask some of them if they'd be willing to share the work. Maybe we'd be able to get it done before closing time today.

T. Well, I guess that'd be O.K. I really don't care how it gets done, just so that it gets done by Monday.

C. Fine. Just leave the orders here and I'll check with the other guys. Can we stop now? I just wanted to tell you that I changed it a little from what you said last time, because I'd be really uncomfortable asking him to check it out with the other guys. That would be a little too strong for me.

T. That's O.K. Any way that you want to improvise is fine. How did you feel about it this time?

C. I felt shaky as hell. It was just so unnatural for me to act that way, you know? I'm just not used to it. To tell you the truth, I was a little surprised that I could do it at all, but I guess that that's partly due to the fact that you're not my boss, and I know that you're not going to fire me or anything like that (laughs).

T. I think that you may be partly right, but I still think that it took quite a bit for you to be able to behave assertively, and I think that you must feel a little proud for being able to act that way.

C. Yes, I guess that I do feel a little proud. The real test will be whether or not I can do it when I really need to—when my boss makes his next unreasonable demand.

T. That's true, but I don't want you to feel that you should be able to go out now and climb all over him if he asks you to do something unreasonable. It's taken many years for you to get the way you are, and I think that it would be unrealistic to believe that after one role-playing session you could be a completely changed person. I think that you should try to be assertive if the situation calls for it, and you should be prepared for some failures as well as some successes. It may take a while, but practice makes better. I'd like you to try to keep a record of the situations you get into that call for assertion, regardless of how you react in them. Try to take the time out to write down exactly what happens, so that we can discuss them here, and perhaps act them out, like we did today.

As illustrated by the above interview, role-playing allows the client to give a clearer picture of what goes on in his encounters than merely describing these encounters. Further, as we mentioned before, role-playing allows the client to imitate the assertive behavior of a "model" in a situation which is quite low in threat value. Practicing assertive behaviors learned by role-playing helps the individual become increasingly confident in the encounters which were previously difficult for him to deal with.

It is important to note that sometimes, people who have difficulty asserting themselves are able to be quite assertive under certain circumstances. When these circumstances are determined, they may provide clues for further treatment. For example, in the interview excerpt just presented, the client was able to be quite assertive when playing the role of his boss. From this discovery, one might begin to hypothesize whether or not he can be assertive when dealing with his subordinates at work, how assertive he is at home, and what there is about the authority implied by being a "boss" that makes him so timid when he has to deal with his boss. Further exploration may have revealed that his father was a very stern, authoritarian kind of a man, who always made the client feel unsure of himself.

Regardless of the client's past history, the role-playing technique can help him to learn to be assertive, and the more he practices, the more comfortable he will be.

One final issue must be discussed. It may seem to many that the approaches described in this chapter and Chapter

10 fail to allow for the fact that people have a certain "nature," and unless that nature is changed, only impermanent superficial changes can be made. Thus, to desensitize a person to a feared situation or to teach a basically timid person to be assertive by role-playing may seem to be aimed at superficial changes that have little to do with the true or deep nature of the individual. We take vehement exception to this point of view. To posit "true" nature, which lies at the core of the client's being and must first be understood by the psychotherapist and then changed to reduce the fears of self-assertion, not only contradicts volumes of research data, but provides a handy "cop-out" for client and therapist alike. It relieves the client of his responsibility for his life, passes it into the hands of the therapist, and sets up a treatment situation that could last for many years and produce no observable change in the client other than an increased knowledge of psychological jargon.

The individual who understands why he is terrified of a certain situation but continues to have the fear cannot be seen as a therapeutic success. Rather, it is more important that the fear be eliminated. True "understanding" of an individual may prove to be a hopeless, endless wild goose chase, and the pursuit of such knowledge may do more to impede the necessary changes in the client than to facilitate them.

Man behaves according to the ways in which he has learned through imitation of others, by formal learning and experience, and by the perspectives from which his thoughts are formulated. The client, then, under the guidance of the therapist, must concentrate on unlearning old, unsuccessful patterns of behavior, and relearning new, more successful modes; the therapist must help his client gain new perspectives from which to view the world. In this way, the client takes the responsibility for changing his own manner of handling himself in the world.

CHAPTER 12

The Client-Therapist Relationship: Cutting the Ties

The therapeutic relationship is saturated with ideas and feelings. However, the ideas and the content of what is discussed are only a small part of the total experience. Perhaps the feelings evoked or remembered as a result of therapy are most important. In previous chapters, feelings concerning the individual's family, past, and specific problems have been exemplified, but the feelings that usually cause confusion are the client's feelings about the therapist.

Upon entering therapy, the client's initial feeling is a mixture of hope, fear and anxiety. Normally, the client believes that the therapist can help to reduce or relieve the psychological pain that he is experiencing, but he also experiences anxiety because he is unsure of what will happen and what will be expected of him. Questions arise, such as, "Can he help me? Should I really be in therapy? If he can't help me, what will become of my life?" These questions and doubts are to be expected in most cases.

While most people overcome these intial fears, intense and confusing feelings often crop up during psychotherapy. One of the emotional responses that may develop is anger directed against the therapist, or perhaps distaste for him. A glance at some things that make the psychotherapy relationship unique is necessary to understand this response to the therapist.

The therapist allows the client to see himself as he affects others, but in a safe environment. Thus, even if the client makes a statement that most polite persons would not pursue or respond to for fear of hurting the client's feelings, the therapist is apt to be quite direct in pointing out how the client is making him feel. He may say that he feels angry at the client, he may accuse the client of seeking sympathy through his actions or statements, and he may not allow the client to use comfortable (yet maladaptive) techniques of relating.

The shock of experiencing this kind of relationship with the therapist often evokes a negative reaction towards the person to whom he has come for help. His mind produces thoughts such as, "I didn't come here and pay this man to insult me"; or "If that's what I get when I talk, I'll just shut up." Again, however, these reactions must be expected because of the nature of this relationship. But if the therapist should not behave as described, the client would gain very little. Anger, frustration, and disappointment are, therefore, expected feelings in regard to a therapist. Most therapists expect the client to feel these emotions and are sensitive to them, but if they are not sensed, it is of utmost importance that the client make it known that he is angry and frustrated. In this way, both parties will gain by understanding one another better, and the therapeutic process will be advanced.

"I'm Not Getting Anywhere"

Most persons have the idea that psychotherapy is a time- and money-consuming process, but this need not be the case. The length of therapy depends on several factors. First, the therapist's orientation is important. Traditionally, therapists who are psychoanalytically oriented probe deep into a person's psychological makeup and spend much time (often years) in the therapeutic process. If one ascribes to this theoretical framework and if a client can afford the time and money, this method can be helpful.

Advocates of other schools of psychotherapy, however, may see the therapy process differently and feel that long periods of treatment are not necessary or appropriate. A majority of psychotherapists believe that the length of therapy depends upon the client as an individual and the nature of his problem rather than on theoretical requirements. This discussion is designed to explain the impatience and dissatisfaction that is another common reaction toward the therapist. In the case of an ear infection, a physician can tell a patient with fair accuracy that it will take two or three days for the pain to abate and that the ear will be completely free of infection after a ten-day course of medication. The psychotherapist cannot make such promises. The reasons for this are that the therapist rarely knows at the outset how long therapy will take or even if it will succeed. He can only assume that if he and the client can relate to one another in a meaningful, emotional way, the client will change—how fast or slow is a matter of pure speculation.

The client, then, cannot look forward to a specific date when he will be "cured"; he will be better "someday." Most clients can accept this uncertainty for a while, but when things get tough, and session after session seems strained and fruitless, he may begin to think that he is making no progress at all. His response will depend on his own personality, his actual therapeutic movement, and his relationship to the therapist. He may, for example, react by accusing the therapist: "You're not helping me. All you do is sit there and listen, but you're not making me any different." Here, the client's belief that he can be changed without involving himself personally is brought to the surface. His therapist will quickly clarify this misconception and talk with the patient about why he reacted at that particular point.

On the other hand, the client may blame himself for his feelings: "I can't change. I'm trying to talk to you and listen to you, but I can't change." Here, the client is attempting to justify his desire to get out of therapy by telling the therapist "You tried and I thank you for it, but it's me. I take all the blame for the failure." Again, the sensitive therapist will discuss this reaction and use it to therapeutic advantage.

Requestioning the therapist about how long therapy might take is another common reaction at this point. The therapist will recognize that his client is becoming anxious about his progress and will discuss the situation with him. Very often, the therapist will explain that impatience for change may indicate that the client is approaching the critical point at which he must commit himself to changing and is having second thoughts about whether or not he really wants to be a different person. The accusation that "nothing's happening" is designed to justify the client's desire to stop treatment before he really has to face up and change himself.

The client's desire for termination, however, is an important component of the emotions that are evoked in psychotherapy. No matter how anxious, lonely or uncomfortable a person may be and how much he wants psychotherapy to help him find relief, there is always some part of a person that wants to resist change. An anxious, unhappy person may be miserable but when he wakes up in the morning, he is sure of who he is and can predict how his day will progress with reasonable accuracy. In spite of his discomfort and unhappiness, the person is "himself." Waking up one morning a new person sounds like an exciting event; actually, it is a frightening prospect.

This, then, is one of the dilemmas confronting the client —he wishes desperately to be rid of the problems and feelings for which he sought help, but he is extremely frightened by the thought of actually being different. He knows how people respond to him when he acts as he does now, and although those reactions are not pleasant, he may worry that things will be worse if he changes. Psychotherapy is directed at changing this "self." The therapist forces the client to face his fears, but encourages him: "Change slowly and hold onto your present self until you can experiment with your new self and be assured that it is more comfortable."

"Let Me Go But Hold Me"

As therapy proceeds successfully and the client experiences positive change, both participants contemplate the possibility of terminating the relationship. The therapist is increasingly concerned with whether or not his client has changed sufficiently and is ready to assume full responsibility for successful functioning and positive emotional growth. The client, on the other hand, is beginning to experience mixed feelings.

The client can be overcome by the feeling that he no longer needs the therapist—that he has put in enough time and money and can go it alone. This idea arouses other reactions, however. The therapist is the "expert" and should tell him when he is well enough to terminate therapy, but perhaps the therapist has not done so. The client may become angry and believe that he is being kept in treatment so that the therapist will not lose a fee. On the other hand, he may think that his progress was less advanced than he had estimated.

As the client approaches the end of treatment, however, a conflict arises. Has he actually changed, or is he only different insofar as his dealings with the therapist? He begins to be afraid to terminate the relationship and either avoids the subject or reacts to it with anxiety. The recurrence of anxiety at this late time in therapy is often misinterpreted by the client as a relapse of his problems. He is afraid that his positive feelings and improved functioning are not real. Perhaps he thinks he is still the same troubled person. All these feelings should be brought out into the open, for they are an important clue to the therapist that the termination phase of therapy has been, or should be, entered.

It is quite understandable and should be expected that the client will be hesitant to let go of the therapist after having him there to help him and listen to his problems during the course of treatment. But both the client and the therapist realize that their relationship is no longer critically important for the client's well-being. Extended treatment would probably result in the client's unnecessary dependence on the therapist and could even terminate in an antitherapeutic relationship. When the client's problems have been brought under control, there is really very little basis for the therapist-client relationship; it cannot be maintained on a social level and must end.

Different agreements may be reached as to the exact nature of the dissolution. The therapist may begin by increasing the time between meetings. If they met once a week, he might increase the intervals to twice a month, then once a month, and so forth. In this way, the client gets to try his own wings for a while with the realization that he is not really out of therapy and will get to talk things out with the therapist after a period of time.

In some cases actual, formal termination may not occur; the client may see the therapist two or three times a year just for a progress report or for a little encouragement, and this pattern may continue indefinitely. Or the relationship might actually come to a formal close. A last session will be held, the participants will bid each other farewell, and the relationship will be completely terminated. Even in this instance, however, the client is always free to contact the therapist at a later time if the need arises. If the therapist then thinks that the client is experiencing more difficulty than would normally be expected, the relationship might be resumed.

This chapter has attempted to present some of the feelings evoked in therapy which are peculiar to the therapy relationship per se. They are reactions to being in therapy more than they are feelings associated with any particular problem or difficulty in living. Many psychotherapy patients will experience all of them and all clients will experience some of them. The important point, however, is that when they are felt they must be brought into the open—they must be verbalized. All too often, clients feel that their negative feelings about the therapist are "wrong" and should not be mentioned. We emphasized, however, that they are to be expected and are integral to the success of therapy. As such, they should be dealt with as deeply and thoroughly as those feelings associated with the client's original problem.

Suggested Reading

Ellis, A. *Reason and emotion in psychotherapy.* New York: Lyle Stuart, 1962.

Eysenck, H. J. (Ed.) *Behavior therapy and the neuroses.* New York: Pergamon, 1960.

Goffmann, E. *Asylums.* Garden City, N.Y.: Doubleday Anchor, 1961.

Goldstein, A. P., Heller, R., & Sechrest, L. B. *Psychotherapy and the psychology of behavior change.* New York: Wiley, 1966.

London, P. *The modes and morals of psychotherapy.* New York: Holt, 1964.

Masters, W., & Johnson, H. *Sexual inadequacy.* Boston: Little, Brown, 1970.

Phillips, E. L., & Wiener, D. N. *Short-term psychotherapy and structured behavior change.* New York: McGraw-Hill, 1966.

Rogers, C. R. *On becoming a person: A therapist's view of psychotherapy.* Boston: Houghton Mifflin, 1961.

Schofield, W. *Psychotherapy: The purchase of friendship.* Englewood Cliffs, N.J.: Prentice-Hall, 1964.

Stein, M. (Ed.) *Contemporary psychotherapies.* New York: Free Press, 1961.

Sullivan, H. S. *The psychiatric interview.* New York: Norton, 1954.

Ullmann, L. P., & Krasner, L. (Eds.) *Case studies in behavior modification.* New York: Holt, 1965.

Wolpe, J. *Psychotherapy by reciprocal inhibition.* Stanford, Calif.: Stanford University Press, 1958.